SANDINISTA

Praise for the series:

It was only a matter of time before a clever publisher realized that there is an audience for whom *Exile on Main Street* or *Electric Ladyland* are as significant and worthy of study as *The Catcher in the Rye* or *Middlemarch* . . . The series . . . is freewheeling and eclectic, ranging from minute rock-geek analysis to idiosyncratic personal celebration — *The New York Times Book Review*

Ideal for the rock geek who thinks liner notes just aren't enough — *Rolling Stone*

One of the coolest publishing imprints on the planet — *Bookslut*

These are for the insane collectors out there who appreciate fantastic design, well-executed thinking, and things that make your house look cool. Each volume in this series takes a seminal album and breaks it down in startling minutiae. We love these. We are huge nerds — *Vice*

A brilliant series . . . each one a work of real love — *NME* (UK)

Passionate, obsessive, and smart — *Nylon*

Religious tracts for the rock 'n' roll faithful — *Boldtype*

[A] consistently excellent series — *Uncut* (UK)

We . . . aren't naive enough to think that we're your only source for reading about music (but if we had our way . . . watch out). For those of you who really like to know everything there is to know about an album, you'd do well to check out Bloomsbury's "33 1/3" series of books — *Pitchfork*

For almost 20 years, the 33-and-a-Third series of music books has focused on individual albums by acts well known (Bob Dylan, Nirvana, Abba, Radiohead), cultish (Neutral Milk Hotel, Throbbing Gristle, Wire) and many levels in-between. The range of music and their creators defines "eclectic", while the writing veers from freewheeling to acutely insightful. In essence, the books are for the music fan who (as Rolling Stone noted) "thinks liner notes just aren't enough." — *The Irish Times*

For reviews of individual titles in the series, please visit our blog at 333sound.com and our website at https://www.bloomsbury.com/academic/music-sound-studies/

Follow us on Twitter: @333books

Like us on Facebook: https://www.facebook.com/33.3books

For a complete list of books in this series, see the back of this book.

Forthcoming in the series:

Shout at the Devil by Micco Caporale
101 by Mary Valle
White Limozeen by Steacy Easton
I'm Wide Awake, It's Morning by Holden Seidlitz
Hounds of Love by Leah Kardos
Re by Carmelo Esterrich
New Amerykah Part Two (Return of the Ankh) by Kameryn Alexa Carter
In the Life of Chris Gaines by Stephen Deusner

and many more . . .

Sandinista!

Micajah Henley

BLOOMSBURY ACADEMIC
NEW YORK • LONDON • OXFORD • NEW DELHI • SYDNEY

BLOOMSBURY ACADEMIC
Bloomsbury Publishing Inc
1385 Broadway, New York, NY 10018, USA
50 Bedford Square, London, WC1B 3DP, UK
29 Earlsfort Terrace, Dublin 2, Ireland

BLOOMSBURY, BLOOMSBURY ACADEMIC and the Diana logo are trademarks of Bloomsbury Publishing Plc

First published in the United States of America 2024

A catalog record for this book is available from the Library of Congress.

ISBN: PB: 978-1-5013-9036-4
ePDF: 978-1-5013-9038-8
eBook: 978-1-5013-9037-1

Series: 33 1/3

Typeset by Deanta Global Publishing Services, Chennai, India
Printed and bound in Great Britain

To find out more about our authors and books visit www.bloomsbury.com and sign up for our newsletters.

Contents

Tracklists

Sandinista Now!

1. Police on My Back
2. Somebody Got Murdered
3. The Call Up
4. Washington Bullets
5. Ivan Meets G.I. Joe
6. Hitsville U.K.
7. Up in Heaven (Not Only Here)
8. The Magnificent Seven
9. The Leader
10. Junco Partner
11. One More Time
12. The Sound of Sinners

Sandinista!

1. The Magnificent Seven
2. Hitsville U.K.

3. Junco Partner
4. Ivan Meets G.I. Joe
5. The Leader
6. Something About England
7. Rebel Waltz
8. Look Here
9. The Crooked Beat
10. Somebody Got Murdered
11. One More Time
12. One More Dub
13. Lightning Strikes (Not Once but Twice)
14. Up in Heaven (Not Only Here)
15. Corner Soul
16. Let's Go Crazy
17. If Music Could Talk
18. The Sound of Sinners
19. Police on My Back
20. Midnight Log
21. The Equaliser
22. The Call Up
23. Washington Bullets
24. Broadway
25. Lose This Skin
26. Charlie Don't Surf

27. Mensforth Hill
28. Junkie Slip
29. Kingston Advice
30. The Street Parade
31. Version City
32. Living in Fame
33. Silicone on Sapphire
34. Version Pardner
35. Career Opportunities
36. Shepherds Delight

Introduction

The Clash's slogan "the only band that matters" was a belief statement shared by many in the late 1970s and early 1980s. Even if they weren't the *only* band that mattered, they were definitely the band that mattered most to their devoted fans. At the very least, they were the band that sang about what mattered most to young fans whose worldviews were challenged by the politics of The Clash. On an episode of the podcast, *You Made It Weird with Pete Holmes*, comedian and musician Fred Armisen told the stand-up, "I believed in The Clash like one believes in a religion."[1] Armisen's statement is true for many people who discovered the punk rock pioneers at an early age. In 2020, photographer Sam Jones conducted an interview with Armisen in which they both describe The Clash as being unlike other bands from their era because their music offered instructions on how to live. Armisen explains that seeing The Clash perform in New York in 1982 still inspires the way he works. Witnessing the band arrive at the venue without a limousine and inviting Armisen and other kids backstage after the show demonstrated to him how to be a performer. During the interview, both named *Sandinista!* as their favorite album of all time. Armisen even shares how the album's experimental nature and even the humor of the triple LP informed his work on the sketch show *Portlandia*.[2] While many Clash fans would agree the band served as a sort of great awakening, even die-hard Clash fans are typically split into two categories: those who believe *Sandinista!* is a masterpiece and those who think it's an absolute mess that's far too long.

Upon its release, *Sandinista!* received mixed reviews, with the harshest criticisms at the time of its release coming from Britain. Nick Kent at *NME* called it "ridiculously self-indulgent" while criticizing guitarist and producer Mick Jones for the mix and suggesting that his vocals, along with Joe Strummer's, are lacking in range and authenticity. Likewise, he criticized Strummer's lyrics as cliché rallying cries. Worst of all, Kent wondered who The Clash's UK audience even was at that point in their career while questioning why they chose to continue being a band. Patrick Humphries at *Melody Maker* described it as a "floundering mutant" of an album that was ultimately a disappointing follow up to *London Calling*. Humphries also accused the title of "reeking of political awareness," similar to how one might critique "wokeness" today. On the other hand, Robbi Millar at *Sounds* wrote that the highs are high and the lows downright puzzling, yet she rated the album with four out of five stars. In America, Robert Christgau called it their worst album while praising them and grading the record with an A– review: "if this is their worst—which it is, I think—they must be, er, the world's greatest rock and roll band." It also placed at the top of *The Village Voice* Pazz and Jop year-end critic's poll, ahead of *Wild Gift* by X, *Trust* by Elvis Costello and The Attractions, and *Controversy* by Prince. Its most glowing review came from John Piccarella in *Rolling Stone*, who said it was the album that saved him from the depression that followed John Lennon's murder just three days before the album's initial release, becoming the first of many to call *Sandinista!* the punk rock equivalent of *The White Album*.

Music fans frequently debate the merits of double LPs. Not even The Beatles' 1968 self-titled album, commonly known as *The White Album*, is exempt from the popular critique: *Could it have been better if it were reduced to a single LP?* Surely, slashing the thirty tracks of *The White Album* would diminish its magnum opus status. At the same time, the endless fascination with the record's cornucopian scale is sustained by the ability to break it apart and reconstruct it. For example, those who favor the songs of John Lennon or Paul McCartney can put together separate solo albums using *White Album* tracks and come out with two new, solid albums. Or one can simply start trimming the fat—beginning with "Piggies"—to create their idea of the "perfect" Beatles record. In the subsequent eras of mixtapes, CD burning, and playlisting, the potential to reimagine *The White Album* has only evolved and expanded. In fact, the album's cover invites this level of fan interaction, acting as a nearly blank 12" x 12" canvas for psychedelic imagery, fanatic engravings, and amateur sketches. The album has even been renamed by those who have loved and debated it. Who sincerely refers to it as *The Beatles*? Few double albums are untouchable, namely *Blonde on Blonde* (1966), *Songs in the Key of Life* (1976), or *Sign 'O' the Times* (1987), otherwise almost no double LP is safe from deconstruction. To be sure, music lovers become much more critical of albums with extensive tracklists, especially when the number of discs increases. *Is this worth my time? Is this worth the extra money? Did they really think all of this was worthy of being released? All of it?*

With The Beatles producing the most beloved and debated double LP, it is fitting that the first rock triple LP is George Harrison's first solo album, *All Things Must Pass* (1970). With twenty-three tracks, the album clocks out around the 106-minute mark, making it only thirteen minutes longer than *The White Album* despite having seven fewer tracks. The triple LP suits the first solo effort by the quiet Beatle, who clearly had a lot to get out after playing third fiddle to the Lennon-McCartney songwriting machine, and it was satisfying for the album's early listeners to hear Harrison finally become untethered with the help of Wall of Sound architect Phil Spector. The first two discs deliver eighteen songs that could have fit on any of the last three Beatles records but are surely best served on *All Things Must Pass.* The third LP, however, is George flexing his musical prowess and consists of almost exclusively improvised instrumental tracks that are subtitled, "Apple Jam." The indulgence of the third LP both pushes the boundaries of the rock album and becomes the key critique of such ambition.

Following *All Things Must Pass*, the triple LP was typically a byproduct of compilations and live albums. The soundtrack to *Woodstock* was released the same year, and only a year later, Harrison and Spector would team up again for *The Concert for Bangladesh* (1971). Naturally, the long-winded format would be adopted by the excessive aesthetics of progressive rock. In 1973, Yes released their platinum-selling live album,

Yessongs. The following year, Emerson, Lake, and Palmer would release their second live album, *Welcome Back My Friends to the Show That Never Ends—Ladies and Gentlemen* (1974). By 1976, Paul McCartney and Wings released *Wings Across America*. Breaking from the live album trope, prog duo Godley & Creme boldly released their 1977 debut *Consequences*, a triple LP that incorporates elements of a stage play, fully embracing the prospects of combining rock and theater. However, the album was also officially released in truncated ten- and eight-track versions. Of course, there's the soundtrack to the Martin Scorsese concert film about The Band's final performance, *The Last Waltz* (1978), which is no match to the movie itself, yet is still an exceptional live document of some of the greatest musicians of the decade.

Which nearly brings us to The Clash. Released a year before *Sandinista!*, Johnny Lydon's Public Image Ltd released what many consider to be a post-punk masterpiece, *Metal Box* (1979). Unlike other triple LPs, *Metal Box* has a humble runtime of just over an hour long, which would typically be better suited for a double LP were it not for it being played at 45 rpm, rather than the standard 33 ⅓ rpm. Finally, in the same year *Sandinista!* was released, Maryland art punks Half Japanese released their triple LP debut, *1/2 Gentlemen/Not Beasts* (1980). Finishing around 133 minutes with thirty-eight songs, it's the album that most resembles The Clash's, though the lo-fi production is more similar to The Clash's *Vanilla Tapes* demos for *London Calling* than *Sandinista!* Overall, *1/2 Gentlemen/Not Beasts* is mostly a composite of original songs bursting for nearly 2 minutes, conjuring the abrasive experimentation of The Velvet

Underground's *White Light/White Heat* (1968), mixed with some unlikely covers from Bob Dylan and Bruce Springsteen, climaxing with two sprawling live tracks that might be described as avant-core. If not for *Sandinista!*, *1/2 Gentleman/ Not Beasts* might be punk's most beloved six-sided artifact.

The fact that a punk band such as The Clash would make a double LP (*London Calling*), followed by a triple LP (*Sandinista!*), risked contradicting the early punk ethos. In the mid- to late 1970s, punk music existed as an antithesis to classic rock bands who played extended solos, be it guitar, drums, or worst of all, synthesizer, on records whose pursuits would eventually be satirized in *This Is Spinal Tap* (1984). Double albums like Led Zeppelin's *Physical Graffiti* (1975), with sprawling arena rock epics like "Kashmir" or the 11-minute endurance test "In My Time of Dying," are prime sources of the burgeoning punk scene's antithetical ire. Just a year later, the Ramones would release their debut album that finishes after just twenty-nine minutes, which is only seven minutes longer than the three songs on side one of *Physical Graffiti*. Oddly enough, the self-titled Ramones album is only one song shorter than Zeppelin's eighty-two-minute double LP.

Conceptually, the objective of punk rock was to cut to the chase. This faction of rock music was not meant to be "progressive" or virtuosic like their prog counterparts, rather it was meant to be raw, primal, and confrontational from start to finish. Look no further than *Never Mind the Bollocks, Here's the Sex Pistols* (1977). The suggestive title and the band itself made statements that were well beyond the self-congratulatory and even masturbatory expressions of larger-than-life rock stars whose talents were too often elevated to hero or divine status. Instead, the Sex Pistols spoke directly to their audience by shouting "forget the bullshit, here's the cultural revolution." Most obviously, the use of obscenity ("bollocks") is intended to be confrontational. Not only does it simultaneously grab your attention and offend the more conservative (and primarily British) observers, it speaks the language of ordinary people. In other words, the Sex Pistols are not there to be viewed as the rock gods, celebrities, or royalty they openly thumb their noses at. Rather, they are every day, working-class people speaking to the populace with a shared language. Lastly, it is a putdown for the current state of rock music that also offers a solution by extending two options: rubbish or punk. As a matter of fact, when the band was battling with the courts over the obscenity of the title, Johnny Rotten quipped, "Don't worry. If we lose the case, we'll retitle the album *Never Mind the Stones, Here's the Sex Pistols*." The joke being that "bollocks" and "stones" were interchangeable euphemisms for testicles, with the bonus of being explicit about their takedown of legacy acts like the Rolling Stones.

Just five months before the Sex Pistols' album, The Clash released their first single "White Riot" with the notable B-side "1977," where Joe Strummer exclaims "No Elvis, Beatles, or the Rolling Stones in 1977!" At this point, The Beatles had long been broken up, and the Rolling Stones were a year away from inserting themselves back into relevance with *Some Girls* (1978) by bending to the will of disco with hits like "Miss You." Almost five months later to the day, however, Elvis Presley died, and rock's so-called "King" was laid to rest in the Southern kingdom he had built for himself in Graceland. Perhaps this validated the young British punks who were creating a cultural movement that had no need for a king. But that didn't stop them from appropriating the design of Elvis' first album for their iconic third record.

The Clash's earliest concept for following up their sophomore album, *Give 'Em Enough Rope* (1978), was titled *The Last Testament*. It was going to be the rock album to end rock. Eventually titled *London Calling*, the double LP called back to only seven years earlier when The Rolling Stones released their ode to American roots music, *Exile on Main St.* (1972), exalting genres like the blues, gospel, swing, country, and early rock 'n' roll. In the same manner, The Clash used the double LP format to explore genres well beyond the limitations and rules of what was decidedly "punk." However, the roots of The Clash varied greatly from that of the Stones. Their ode to rockabilly was a cover of "Brand New Cadillac" by England's own Vince Taylor. What the band may not have known was that David Bowie's alter ego Ziggy Stardust was inspired directly from Taylor, which Bowie revealed in interviews later in life. While The Clash's roots may not have been as historically deep as the Stones', they did have a wider reach. To a lesser degree, *London Calling* still manages to evoke the American South with "Hateful," conjuring the sounds of New Orleans R&B, which borrows rhythmically from Caribbean music traditions. Meanwhile, tracks like "Jimmy Jazz" evoke a punk rock take on lounge music while simultaneously serving as an ode to reggae legend Jimmy Cliff and the highly influential film soundtrack to *The Harder They Come* (1972), which included the Toots and The Maytals track

"Pressure Drop" that The Clash covered. Tracks like "Rudie Can't Fail" and "Wrong 'Em Boy" wear their ska influence on their sleeves, while the most straightforward reggae sendup, "The Guns of Brixton," is led by bassist Paul Simonon who grew up in the titular district in South London.

The influence of reggae was nothing new for The Clash. Their debut album featured a cover of Junior Murvin's "Police and Thieves," produced by dub music pioneer Lee "Scratch" Perry, who produced The Clash's 1977 single "Complete Control" after their label released "Remote Control" as a single without consulting the band. What came as a surprise was the Phil Spector–inspired production of "The Card Cheat" that closes side three of *London Calling*, but unlike the Ramones, who famously worked with Spector on their album *End of the Century* (1980), they didn't resort to bubblegum lyrics for the sake of pastiche or irony. The biggest surprise of a track on *London Calling* is probably "Train in Vain (Stand by Me)." The song was especially surprising to the album's earliest listeners because the title doesn't appear on either the back cover or the label on side four, but what's most jarring for Clash fans of the time is the straightforward pop nature of the track. Rather than being a socially or politically charged romp led by Strummer, Mick Jones takes over on vocals to croon about heartbreak after his relationship with The Slits guitarist Viv Albertine came to an end. The Clash's clean break from punk rock purity allowed "Train in Vain" to reach the Top 30 after being released as a single.

With its visual reference to Elvis, successful single, experimentation with other genres, and nineteen songs spread across two LPs, *London Calling* challenged the very idea of what punk meant in relation to recorded music. Almost exactly a year later, they would take that even further with a triple LP, *Sandinista!* While the format may resemble the prog predecessors, *Sandinista!* is unlike anything that came before it, including Public Image Ltd.'s own *Metal Box*. But what makes *Sandinista!* an exceptional work isn't just that there are three discs with a total of thirty-six songs that finish at the 144-minute mark. Only four years later, *Double Nickels on the Dime* by Minutemen would reach forty-five tracks with a double LP. What truly separates *Sandinista!* from other large and ambitious works is that it is a continuation of the band's deviation from the punk genre, displaying their ability to adopt everything from hip-hop, jazz, and folk, to calypso, rockabilly, reggae, and dub. More than any album of theirs, it also ties them to England, America (specifically New York), Jamaica, and Central America, as suggested by the title's reference to the Sandinista National Liberation Front (FSLN) in Nicaragua.

The first and most obvious message of *Sandinista!* is that the band does not belong to a singular musical scene or genre, or even a geographical place. The band, and this album, exists for anyone and everyone who will listen. On the other hand, it is an album that exists as a subversive act against both Thatcherism and the newly elected president Ronald Reagan. Margaret Thatcher attempted to ban the word "Sandinista" after the militant socialists overthrew the violently oppressive Somoza dynasty. Similarly, Reagan would announce only a few years later, "I am a Contra," adopting the name of the right-wing terrorist organization who opposed the newly formed Sandinista government.

While the album invites music listeners of all kinds, it also serves as an act of resistance toward the growing conservative movements in England and the United States.

At worst, critics questioned whether the band should stay together. At best, the record was compared to a Beatles classic. For the most part, initial reviews and more recent revaluations are split, with the latter deeming the album a flawed masterpiece. Author and biographer Tony Fletcher agrees that *Sandinista!* is a "sprawling, confused, overly ambitious, frequently self-indulgent and yet occasionally brilliant work of madness," yet he argues its "over-indulgence and under-production is also its triple triumph."[3] Music writer David Quantick argues that the album's length and inconsistency in terms of great songs ultimately makes it unsuccessful while pitching a collection of songs for a 90-minute mixtape version that scraps the filler.[4] In his book, *The Clash: The Only Band That Mattered*, Sean Egan writes, "There had never been truly awful material on Clash records before, but its presence here was not the signpost of an artistic downslide: as a single album, *Sandinista!* would have been a classic."[5]

Because the album is so frequently referred to as an imperfect masterpiece in need of being shortened, this book entertains that theory by looking at the twelve-track promo version of the album, *Sandinista Now!*, as an alternative to the original triple LP. The aim of this book is to look at the promo and determine if it is a satisfactory—or even superior—alternate version for those who deem the original album excessive. To do this, Part I is divided into two chapters, each dedicated to one side of the promo record, discussing each song from either a historical, analytical, or critical perspective. Part II of the book looks at the remaining tracks on the record by devoting a chapter to each of the three LPs to evaluate the tracks absent from the shorter version.

To be sure, truly great albums are typically more than a record with a great set of songs. There are historical reasons why a record can be important. Many of the canonized "greatest albums of all time" are the first to accomplish something in terms of production, sales, or intent. Many albums are elevated by an iconic cover (*The Velvet Underground & Nico*, *The Dark Side of the Moon*). Others are marked by the story that comes with them. Admittedly, many fans enjoy Wilco's *Yankee Hotel Foxtrot* (2002) more because it was the album that got them dropped by Reprise, the one that is the first for Glenn Kotche and last for Jay Bennett, the one that streamed online a week after 9/11 featuring a cover of two identical towers with tracks like "Ashes of American Flags," and because most of that was captured in the contemporaneous documentary, *I Am Trying to Break Your Heart* (2002). Similarly, *Sandinista!* is best appreciated when considering that the band fought with their label to sell the triple LP for the price of one for the sake of their fans. To do so, they agreed to pay the difference out of what they would have earned from the royalties.

The book concludes by arguing that *Sandinista!* would not have been better if it were reduced to twelve tracks. On the other hand, once the thirty-six tracks belong to the fans, it is up to them to do with them what they will. The excessive nature of the album invites discourse, forcing debates among fans and critics. More than that, it urges fans to devise their own versions of the album to be shared, offering different perspectives and approaches, and creating new appreciation for songs that were otherwise ignored. The album is built for this type of active engagement. That is the strength of *Sandinista!* and why it is another of The Clash's masterworks. For this reason, the book ends with a collection of twelve-track versions of *Sandinista!* created by myself, friends, musicians, writers, and other Clash fans.

But before an examination of the album begins, it would be beneficial to discuss the politics of Joe Strummer and The Clash. In particular, Joe Strummer has been referred to as a Marxist, socialist, revolutionary, and more based on his lyrics and statements on and off stage. Since *Sandinista!* is often considered to be The Clash's most political album, it follows that a clear understanding of Strummer's political beliefs should be explored before applying them to the content of these thirty-six songs. To do this, Strummer's ideas will be compared to those of Marxist writer Ernst Fischer, particularly his book *The Necessity of Art* (1959). Though Strummer's beliefs can be heard or read about in his lyrics and the various interviews from his lifetime, they can be difficult to understand since Strummer himself cared very little about how to properly identify his own beliefs. Regardless, echoes of Fischer's writing can be found in the words of Joe Strummer, despite the fact he potentially never read or even heard of Ernst Fischer. In any case, Fisher's understanding of art and socialism helps to dissect what Strummer believed and felt, even if he couldn't always articulate it himself.

1
The Politics of the Clash

In his book *The Necessity of Art: A Marxist Approach*, Austrian writer-politician Ernst Fischer makes the case for the social significance of art. He writes, "Art is the indispensable means for this merging of the individual with the whole. It reflects his infinite capacity for association for sharing experiences and ideas."[1] This agreeable statement can be applied to any form of art, but it feels especially true for music, and no more so than with The Clash. When it comes to "merging the individual with the whole," The Clash's appeal as a live act was rooted in their ability to connect with their audience and blur the line between the stage and concert floor. In his essay on various Clash concerts between 1977 and 1982, Peter Smith describes the band's early shows as having the ability to break what he refers to as the Fifth Wall—"that which divided those outside the venues, and wishing to gain entrance, from those inside the hall attending the concert."[2] There are multiple accounts of The Clash sneaking in fans through dressing room doors and windows, and various other means of bringing people in who didn't have tickets or couldn't afford them. All these examples demonstrate the band's attempt to merge with their audience and rectify social and economic inequalities. Regarding "sharing experiences and ideas," that was a clear objective of The Clash. In his essay, "Politics, Pastiche, Parody and Polemics: The DIY Educational Inspiration of The Clash," Andy Zieleniec argues, "The Clash offered new ways of thinking about politics and the world, providing information and inspiration about and of wider social, historical, economic and political processes,"[3] which might partially explain the vast, generous size of *Sandinista!*

After exploring the origins of humanity's fascination and need for art, Fischer discusses the concept of "socialist realism"—a realistic style of art developed by the Soviet Union after the Second World War promoting communist values—and his dissatisfaction with the term. He explains that socialist realism "has frequently been abused and misapplied to academic historical and genre paintings and to novels and plays in fact based on propagandist idealizations. For this reason . . . the term 'socialist art' seems to me to be better. It clearly refers to an attitude—not style—and emphasizes the socialist outlook, not the realist method."[4] What's interesting about applying Fischer's ideas to The Clash is how Joe Strummer echoes his remarks as it relates to the punk movement of the 1970s: "Punk rock isn't something you grow out of. Punk rock is an attitude, and the essence of that attitude is 'give us some truth.'" To be sure, style is an important tenet of punk culture. As a matter of fact, Mick Jones recruited Paul Simonon because of his fashion sense, despite the fact that he couldn't play bass upon joining The Clash. But this attitude of "passion over precision" is what makes punk appealing and accessible to working-class youth. Moreover, the quote from Strummer also resembles a classic track from John Lennon's solo career, "Gimme Some Truth." The key difference between Strummer's and Lennon's remarks is that Lennon wants the truth for himself and cries "give *me* some truth," while Strummer opens it up to "us."

Strummer's idea of punk being about a particular attitude in pursuit of truth is what set The Clash apart from other acts, namely the Sex Pistols. Early in the band's career, Strummer proclaimed, "We're anti-fascist, we're anti-violence, we're anti-racist, and we're pro-creative. We're against ignorance." Meanwhile, the Sex Pistols embraced a more nihilistic worldview in claiming, "there's no future." According to Fischer, "the nihilist artist is generally not aware he is, in effect, surrendering into the hands of the capitalist bourgeois world."[5] Conversely, Fischer writes, "Socialist realism—or rather, socialist art—anticipates the future."[6] Unlike the Sex Pistols, The Clash were majorly influenced by reggae music. The appeal of reggae was that it was rebel music that expressed Rastafarian beliefs in hope for the future, expressing joy for the eventual destruction of Babylon, the Rasta understanding of colonialism and imperialism in relation to the African diaspora. In his essay "Turning Rebellion into Money: The Roots of The Clash," Lloyd I. Vayo insists that punk rock, like reggae, could similarly be used to "critique the world around them, its failings, and the path forward into a better world to come."[7] It's worth noting that *Sandinista!* contains more reggae and dub tracks than any Clash album before or after it.

The parallels between Fischer and Strummer don't automatically constitute The Clash as a socialist band, or *Sandinista!* as a piece of socialist art. But for his part,

Strummer was a self-professed socialist with a worldview shaped by socialist beliefs. He explained, "I believe in socialism because it seems more humanitarian, rather than every man for himself and 'I'm alright, Jack' and all those asshole businessmen with all the loot. I made up my mind from viewing society from that angle. That's where I'm from and there's where I've made my decisions from."[8] This proclamation may not be sufficient for some since it is mostly personal and doesn't outright describe his position on economic power structures as much as his dislike for "businessmen with all the loot." Above all else, Strummer was a musician, not a politician or an economist, and the revolution waged by Strummer and The Clash was in the sphere of popular culture. Yet they brought revolutionary politics into music, and this is still of great importance—even if that revolution was being communicated in ways that were, as Gregor Gall writes, "broad, if not also ill-defined."[9]

To be sure, Strummer promoted what was perceived and, therefore, considered to be socialist ideals in his music and performances. No one has done more to understand Strummer's politics and how they evolved over time than Gall in his book *The Punk Rock Politics of Joe Strummer*. In the book, Gall describes Strummer's socialist worldview as incomprehensive, inconsistent, and even incoherent. After doing exhaustive research on Strummer's intellectual history, Gall concludes, "Strummer was not a revolutionary socialist or Marxist as defined by [activist Hal] Draper's 'socialism from below.' Instead, he was more of a reformist socialist, combining elements of Maoism and social democracy with aversion to political parties, thereby giving his socialist beliefs anarchist and libertarian tinges."[10] To be clear, this is not how Strummer defined his own beliefs. In fact, these hairsplitting designations are something Strummer would undoubtedly have no interest in since, again, he was an artist and not a political theorist.

Gall also makes a distinction between social realism and socialist realism, and how Strummer's views can be evaluated by these distinctions. He explains that social realism is "an artistic approach describing, reflecting or representing the manifest economic, social and political conditions of not just workers and the working class but exploited and oppressed groups under capitalism."[11] Anyone familiar with even a handful of Clash songs should be able to apply these characteristics to any number of songs. On the other hand, Gall writes that socialist realism "makes a call to act," not to just "campaign or ameliorate the effects of capitalism but also to take steps to abolish capitalism itself."[12] By his own admission, Strummer had no plans to save the world, saying, "I believe in the socialist way. I don't know any more than that. I don't know any system to save the world, but I believe that socialism at least has more humanity in it."[13] Furthermore, Strummer never had any loyalty to a party or organization. In earlier Clash interviews, Strummer also said, "I don't wanna say I am a socialist or that I am a communist 'cause I fuckin hate parties and party doctrine" and "The Socialist Works Party, you know, they keep coming up to us and saying 'Come on, join us'—but they can fuck off the wankers, that's just dogmas. I don't want no dogma."[14] While Gall interprets this as an anarchist and libertarian edge, one could reasonably believe he was inspired by the Rastafarian rejection of all "isms" in any form—capitalism, socialism, communism, and even Rastafarian*ism*.

Strummer did believe in and promote a particular revolution. By 1984, he was preaching that "Real revolutions take place in the mind."[15] In another interview he added, "I don't believe that an armed revolution is ever an actual revolution. The revolution is in our minds."[16] It's unlikely that he was aware that his beliefs mirror those of American founding father John Adams, who wrote to Thomas Jefferson, "The revolution was in the minds of the people . . . fifteen years before a drop of blood was shed in Lexington."[17] He could have just as easily constructed this new belief on the title of James Brown's *Revolution of the Mind: Live at the Apollo Vol. III* (1971). Regardless, Strummer ultimately believed that the truth was the key to progress, and it was his job to share the truth. Perhaps aware of his limitations as an educator and philosopher, he also encouraged people to pursue the truth for themselves. Strummer claimed The Clash were "encouraging rather than preaching, arousing interest in the likes of say, the Sandinistas, so that people can investigate for themselves."[18] For many, this revolution was gallantly fought and won by The Clash. Musicians, scholars, and fans from all walks of life have testified that The Clash exposed them to ideas that opened them up to the belief that hegemonic society can be challenged and that political and socio-cultural changes are a realistic possibility rather than hippie idealism.

Though Gall has explained the confusion and inconsistencies regarding Strummer's ideas about socialism in its various forms, it still feels necessary to continue tying Strummer to Ernst Fischer, who was deemed a "heretical Marxist" who himself "lacked a model for Socialism," despite his belief that "capitalism would eventually destroy man—or be overthrown."[19] The Clash's most explicit attempt to align themselves with socialism is indeed the title of their fourth album: *Sandinista!* In 1979, the Sandinista National Liberation Front (FSLN) of Nicaragua successfully overthrew the Somoza dynasty that had ruled the country since 1936, establishing the Junta of National Reconstruction in its stead. When asked why the band wanted to name their album after the socialist revolutionaries, Strummer replied,

> For me, it's a very powerful word. And one that people should know because in Nicaragua the Sandinistas have just taken over, and they managed to get rid of a dictatorship, which nobody could say was good. I mean the brutality and torture that was being heaped on them—no one can tell me that's a good thing, you know? And they managed to get rid of it by their own selves, their own actions, you know? They did it themselves while they were being slaughtered and they managed to do it. I think it's a really powerful word, and I wanted to put it about because it's not the kind of thing that papers are printing.[20]

Strummer then describes the title and the album cover, saying, "I just look at it as a space on a piece of paper or bit of cardboard that will be all over the world. I'm proud that our records are heard all over the world. We could have put some groovy phrase . . . or something meaningless, but I wanted to put something that meant something there."[21]

Knowing that the record would be sold all over the world by way of a capitalist industry, the band used their platform to promote the ideals represented by the FSLN. For Strummer, the idea of banding together to fight for yourself and your community and overthrow a dictatorship, then replacing it with something radically new is something that resonated with British and American listeners at the start of Thatcherism and the Reagan Era. However, *Sandinista!* is far from a concept album. The album isn't about the Sandinistas or any one theme. In fact, the titular rebels are only mentioned in one song, "Washington Bullets," which is buried twenty-three songs into the thirty-six tracks. Even that song isn't exclusively about the Sandinistas or Nicaragua. The title does, however, set the tone for the record by emphasizing a recent historical event and considering what's possible for the rest of the world based on the promise of the successful Nicaraguan revolution.

But just naming an album *Sandinista!* and mentioning them by name in "Washington Bullets" doesn't automatically make it a piece of socialist art, just like younger generations shouldn't assume that Vampire Weekend's *Contra* is retroactively supporting the right-wing terrorist organization aided by the US government to overthrow the Sandinistas soon after the release of *Sandinista!* (In actuality, the title was inspired by the 1980s video game *Contra*, although many believe the song "Diplomat's Son" to be a reference to Strummer.) Concerning this question of subject and content—that is, the main object depicted in a work of art versus the overall meaning or intention of the artwork—Fischer writes, "Subject is raised to the status of content only by the artist's attitude, for content is not only what is presented but also how it is presented . . . everything depends on the artist's view, on whether he speaks as an apologist of the ruling class, a sentimental Sunday tripper, a disgruntled peasant, or a revolutionary socialist."[22] Of course, Fischer's writing predates punk rock, so there are some leaps to be made, but with rock LPs being raised to the status of art in the second half of the twentieth century, one could reasonably categorize *Sandinista!* as a work of art or be tempted to go a step further and call it socialist art.

It should be noted that this book is not arguing that punk rock is in and of itself socialist music. To put it plainly, no genre is inherently socialist, and socialist art is not itself a genre. As stated earlier, the label of socialist art relies on the views of the artist, yet this is not the only characteristic of Fischer's definition. Like the punks of the mid- to late 1970s, Fischer was calling for new forms of expression in all types of art "in order to depict new realities."[23] He continues:

> It is doctrinaire to prescribe that socialist art must carry on all forms of bourgeois art, and particularly those of the Renaissance and of nineteenth-century Russian realism. The Renaissance produced magnificent artists; but why should socialist art not also learn from Egyptian or Aztec sculpture, from East Asian drawings and paintings, from Gothic art, from icons, from Manet, Cezanne, Moore, Picasso? The realism of Tolstoy and Dostoyevsky is superb: but why should not the socialist writer also learn from Homer and the Bible, from Shakespeare and Strindberg,

> Stendhal and Proust, Brecht and O'Casey, Rimbaud and Yeats?[24]

Just as Fischer claims socialist art should not rely exclusively on the bourgeois art of the past that most art of his time was rooted in, The Clash and their punk rock contemporaries rejected the established rock tradition that came before them. By the mid- to late 1970s, the legacy acts of the 1960s were institutional "classics" in the rock world, and therefore remnants of the past that The Clash aimed to evolve beyond. Fischer's call for a socialist art that looks to Homer, the Bible, Gothic Art, Aztec sculptures, Shakespeare, and beyond is precisely the nature of *Sandinista!*, which demonstrates The Clash's ability to adopt jazz, calypso, reggae, dub, hip-hop, and gospel music. The message of political-minded punks is not limited to one sound. For it to be an effective and inclusive message, it must be presented in multiple genres.

Looking beyond the rock canon of the previous twenty years, The Clash looked toward Jamaica and the West Indies for inspiration, especially bassist Paul Simonon, who had an affinity for dub and reggae music. On their first album, the band covered reggae artist Junior Murvin's "Police and Thieves." Not only did punk audiences accept it, but reggae artists found allies in the white punk rockers. In response to the punk interpretation of reggae, Bob Marley wrote a song about a "Punky Reggae Party" where The Wailers, The Damned, The Jam, The Clash, The Maytals, and Dr. Feelgood were all invited. Additionally, Lee "Scratch" Perry, who was a co-writer and producer of the original version of "Police and Thieves," produced the first single The Clash released after their debut album, "Complete Control." The success of The Clash's diversity of style comes from the fact that they were not merely trying to imitate style but weld forms of expression, as Fischer proposed. In doing so, they rejected the punk rock dogmatics of the time and ignored the dichotomy of what qualifies as punk and what is decidedly *not* punk.

On *London Calling* (1979) the band had gone beyond punk and even reggae, experimenting with interpretations of early rock 'n' roll ("Brand New Cadillac"), New Orleans R&B ("Hateful"), ska ("Rudie Can't Fail"), and Wall of Sound-style pop music ("The Card Cheat"). As great as *London Calling* is, it is a relatively conventional punk album compared to what follows. On *Sandinista!*, The Clash pushes this further by not only including more reggae tracks and dub tracks but also a tribute to Motown ("Hitsville U.K."), a Cold War–themed dance battle-disco track ("Ivan Meets G.I. Joe"), a cover of jazz and blues pianist Mose Allison ("Look Here"), calypso music ("Let's Go Crazy"), and even a gospel tune ("The Sound of Sinners"). But the most surprising genre that The Clash integrates into their work is hip-hop. The album's first track, "The Magnificent Seven," is a lengthy opener that details a day in the life of a minimum wage worker in a style that was new and potentially foreign to many listeners in punk rock circles, especially those in Britain.

In the end, Fischer argues on behalf of artists, writing that "art does not have to be understood and approved by everyone from the start. It is not the function of art to break down open doors but rather to open locked ones. But when the artist discovers new realities, he does not do so for himself alone; he does it also for others . . . He produces a community."[25] This is precisely the aim of *Sandinista!* The thirty-six songs are meant to unlock doors that lead to new musical styles, different geographic places, political ideals, and, as Fischer puts it, new realities. And this is not for the sake of the band—although Fischer writes, "a composer, as much as any other artist, ultimately serves a social need. But there is also his own individual need as an artist to take pleasure in what he is doing"[26]—the abundance of tracks spanning different genres imagines a new, better world characterized by shared experiences, inclusivity, and cultural exchange. In the words of Fischer,

> it is more likely that a wide variety of styles will be the new characteristic of a culture and age in which nations will merge into one, new syntheses will destroy all that is parochial and static, and no center, either of class or nation, will predominate. In a classless society we are likely to find a multiplicity of styles.[27]

The diversity of genres on *Sandinista!* merges the musical traditions of a multitude of nations to create a transnational opus that is held together by the album's humanist and progressive themes. For some, the range of genres explored on *Sandinista!* isn't the issue. The question is typically: *Why does it have to be this long?* Of course, when asked why they decided to release the album as a triple LP, Strummer quipped, "Just for fun really."[28] In other instances, Strummer said it was to get back at their label for being resistant to releasing *London Calling* as a double LP while allowing Bruce Springsteen to release his own double album, *The River* (1980), presumably without any pushback. Though humorous, it shouldn't be regarded as the primary reason for *Sandinista*'s length. On the other hand, the band did delight in testing how far they could push the limits put on them by their label.

The album isn't designed to test listeners' endurance as much as it is made to challenge people on an epistemological level. In the end, the objective of The Clash was not to change the world but to tell the world that it can be different. As musicians, and not politicians, their means of edification was their music not policymaking. And their music is the only wealth they had to distribute, hence the abundance of wealth that is *Sandinista!* Unknowingly teasing the name of the band that would unknowingly embrace his philosophy, Fischer writes, "freed by the clash of opinion, art that is socialist in its content will—of this I am sure—become richer, bolder, more all-embracing in its themes and forms, its endeavors, and the variety of its movements, than any art of the past."[29] Undoubtedly, The Clash could have squeezed all the genre diversity and political themes onto a single or double LP and still met the criteria for Fischer's definition of socialist art. Yet according to Mick Jones, "You can cut it down if you wanted but you'd miss—it would be missing the point somewhat, I think."[30]

2
The Making of *Sandinista!*

There are a number of things that can help indicate whether an album is "good" or not. If an album sells, it's presumably popular and generally well-liked. On the other hand, if it doesn't sell well, it can achieve something even greater in the world of music lovers—underdog or cult status. Of course, looking at how an album sells is not an evaluation of the actual contents of a record. For a lot of people, a great album is probably one that just has a lot of good songs. At the very least, it should have more good songs than bad or uninteresting ones. Some albums function as a complete statement instead of a collection of singles. Some, like Kate Bush's *Hounds of Love* (1985), manage to do both, making it an album that continues to find new listeners. Albums can also have historical significance for being the first of its kind. First LP, first concept album, first double or triple LP, first to set a record, and so on. Albums that pioneer or define a genre or subgenre are typically highly valued. Likewise, an album that boldly defies genre is also held in high esteem. Finally, great albums can also be defined by the stories surrounding the record.

Stories about an album can propel it to mythic status. Surely part of the appeal of Big Star's *Third* is that it has no official title or release date. It has been called *The Third Album* (UK LP, 1978), *3rd* (US LP, 1978), *Big Star's 3rd: Sister Lovers* (1987), *Third/Sister Lovers* (1992), and *Complete Third* (2016), and each of these has a unique tracklist. Some argue that it isn't even a Big Star record but rather an Alex Chilton solo album or a new band with Chilton and drummer Jody Stephens called Sister Lovers. The deeper you look into it, the more complicated it gets and the more endearing the album becomes. *Sandinista!* shares close to nothing with the third Big Star album, but the fact remains that the narratives music listeners share about an album adds to its value.

The Clash were very conscious mythmakers. Joe Strummer's own origin is comparable to ancient myths and the hero's journey. Despite coming from a middle-class family with a father who worked in the foreign office, Strummer left his metaphorical castle and spent his most formative years squatting in London where he witnessed poverty and racism, further shaping his politics. Like plenty of rock bands, there are stories of how Strummer and Mick Jones met, how Paul Simonon couldn't play bass, how they fired their drummer Terry Chimes and changed his name to "Tory Crimes" on their debut album because he was in it for the money instead of the message. Many of these stories are designed to convince people that The Clash, above all else, have integrity and that they were "the only band that matters."

One of the key figures of The Clash myth and mythmaking is on-again, off-again band manager Bernie Rhodes. It was Rhodes who got Strummer to leave his previous band, the

101ers, and join The Clash. Rhodes acted as the Andy Warhol to their Velvet Underground, helping the band shape their image as a politically minded punk act. The cynics might call him the one who helped construct The Clash "brand." Rhodes also wanted to be considered the fifth member of the band by joining them during interviews and answering questions. As the band became more successful, he wanted to continue enforcing his input. After scheduling the band for a show they had to cancel, The Clash went to personally apologize to the fans for the cancellation and sacked Bernie. The two albums that The Clash made without Rhodes are the apex of their creative output. Both *London Calling* and *Sandinista!* were written, recorded, and released without his heavy hand, whose absence offered The Clash a creative freedom that they otherwise wouldn't have had. Ironically, Strummer insisted Rhodes come back after the release of *Sandinista!* During the recording of *Combat Rock* and subsequent touring, Rhodes fostered conflict between Jones and Strummer, which sadly led to Jones being kicked out of the band. This resulted in the Clash album that most fans don't speak of. *Cut the Crap* (1985) doesn't feature any previous Clash members except Strummer, who shares songwriting credits with Rhodes, who also served as producer under the pseudonym Jose Unidos. Needless to say, Rhodes is a complicated character in The Clash's history. From mentor to mercenary, Rhodes could be deemed one of the most crucial forces behind the band's origin and demise. His absence is also one of the most significant things to happen to the band.

Before Rhodes finally took over as co-songwriter and producer, Clash songs were typically credited to Strummer and Jones. On *Sandinista!*, however, the credit went to The Clash, a symbolic gesture of the band's democratic relationship at the time. Even though drummer Topper Headon was struggling with addiction and Paul Simonon skipped part of the recording sessions to film a movie, there's a tightness on *Sandinista!* that isn't there on other Clash records. There's freedom to play different instruments, experiment in any genre, and even allow Headon and Simonon to write and sing. Not only is it the first Clash album to have the band as the credited songwriter, but it's also the only album credited as being solely produced by The Clash. Jones, in particular, took everything he learned from previous producers Mickey Foote, Sandy Pearlman, and Guy Stevens and produced a Clash album that is perhaps their greatest artistic statement. In addition to Mikey Dread, who co-wrote and produced numerous tracks despite not being properly credited, The Clash also relied heavily on Bill Price, who mixed the album, and the engineers from Electric Lady, Wessex, and Channel One: J.P. Nichols, Jeremy "Jerry" Green, and Lancelot "Maxie" McKenzie.

Though The Clash are the only officially credited writers and producers, the album was the most collaborative effort in their discography. Dread assisted on many tracks and is the primary singer on "Living in Fame." Likewise, Tymon Dogg's violin is heard throughout the record, and his own "Lose This Skin" jumpstarts the album's fifth side. While Simonon was away, Blockheads bassist Norman Watt-Roy filled in, providing the iconic bass line on "The Magnificent Seven" to open the record. Fellow Blockheads bandmate Mickey Gallagher contributes on the keys and has his children appear on two tracks. Davey Payne, also from The Blockheads, contributes on the saxophone, as does Gary Barnacle. There's Ivan Julian from The Voidoids appearing on "The Call Up." And one of the most important contributors was Mick Jones' girlfriend at the time, Ellen Foley, who co-leads "Hitsville U.K." and sings backup on "Corner Soul" and "Washington Bullets." Soon after the release of *Sandinista!*, Foley released a solo album, *Spirit of St. Louis* (1981), which was produced by Jones at Wessex Studios and featured The Clash and other musicians involved in the making of *Sandinista!*, with Strummer and Jones receiving songwriting credits for half of the album's tracks. With so many people in the studio to work on the *Sandinista!*, Strummer had to come up with a way to organize the chaos.

The spliff bunker was an essential part of the writing and recording process at Electric Lady. Jones recalls, "Joe made a bunker for himself in the studio out of flight cases, and then he'd go in to bang out some lyrics then he'd bring them out and I'd sort of do the same for a tune."[1] According to Strummer, "you cannot have people pouring wine into the mixing desk or behaving like that, so I invented the spliff bunker where you could smoke, hang out and talk in the main body of the studio removed geographically from the control room. It was somewhere sanity could reign and people could EQ things correctly."[2] As comical as the idea of a spliff bunker is, The Clash took their jobs seriously and depended on some sense of structure. Recording *London Calling*, the band would experiment in the studio for hours, retire downstairs to play soccer, and then return to work. However, they were also being produced by Guy Stevens, who was a minister of chaos known for throwing chairs and literally pouring wine on the piano. The method for *Sandinista!* was smoke, chill, write, play, and then they would lay the track down in their respective, controlled environments. Knowing this makes some of the better tracks more impressive, and some of the more challenging tracks understandable.

The most outrageous aspect of the album was the band trying to convince CBS to price it as three for the price of one. Knowing that the label pushed back against reducing the price of their previous double LP, the demand to price the triple LP was, as Strummer said, "triply outrageous." According to Jones, they anticipated a pushback from CBS, so they stole the master tapes until they finished negotiating the price. The band initially pitched that the album be sold for £5, which the label refused. CBS settled for selling the triple LP at £5.99 under two conditions. First, the album would only count as one release instead of three, keeping them bound to their CBS contract. Second, the band would have to forgo performance royalties on the first 200,000 copies sold. Band biographer Marcus Gray points out that, at that point, *London Calling* hadn't even sold 200,000 copies in the UK.[3] Nevertheless, The Clash agreed. Meanwhile, American listeners had to pay $14.98, which was less of a bargain than UK listeners got, but still slightly less than a standard double LP.

From a business perspective, this was a bad deal for the band. But The Clash, once again, were able to get a powerful label to honor their demands and provide an affordable product for their fans. While it was bad business, the pricing of *Sandinista!* allowed The Clash to maintain their integrity and punk rock ethos. Concerning the pricing of the record, Strummer said, "The thing I like about taking a stand on prices is that it's *here and now* . . . It's dealing with reality . . . It's one of the few opportunities we have to manifest our ideals," especially during the Thatcher-era recession.[4]

Part I
Sandinista Now!

The main objective of this book is to determine if *Sandinista!* could be improved with a shorter tracklist. The template for this experiment is the *Sandinista Now!* DJ promo that reduces the thirty-six tracks to a humble twelve, complete with an alternate title and packaging. The alternate title immediately recalls Francis Ford Coppola's Vietnam War epic *Apocalypse Now!* (1979). The film is infamous for its chaotic production. In fact, Coppola shot over a million feet of film over the course of the 238 days of principal photography. There are multiple versions of the films with different run-times, making it a fitting title for a would-be Clash LP that is striving for the musical equivalent of what grandiose filmmaking can achieve. Although, it is ironic that the short version of the album has a more epic title.

The album art of *Sandinista Now!* is a plain white backdrop, ironically reminiscent of *The White Album* (1968). The title and the band's name are clumsily stamped on the cover giving it a DIY presentation akin to The Replacements' EP *Stink* (1982) or the many variations of Bob Dylan's *Great*

White Wonder bootlegs. Additionally, DJs received a letter from CBS explaining, "We thought we'd make it easier for you to program a triple album packed with great rock and roll Clashichs." An additional letter informs DJs that the *Gavin Report* trade publication recommended seven of the tracks listed on the promo, as well as "Charlie Don't Surf" and the Mose Allison cover "Look Here." Not only did the label create the twelve-track promo to instruct DJs on how to best program and promote the record, but Robert Christgau even mentions it in his initial review for the record, writing, "Listen to *Sandinista Now!*, the promo-only one-disc digest Epic has thoughtfully provided busy radio personnel."[1] Despite his endorsement of the abridged version, Christgau immediately follows with a short list of his favorite tracks that are missing from the promo.

This nondescript approach to the release of the fourth Clash album could have been a cool move for the pioneering punks who had once entertained the idea of releasing the demos for *London Calling*, also known as *The Vanilla Tapes*, as their third album to make up for their overly polished sophomore release that was panned by punk rock purists. But the minimalist, bootleg-inspired packaging of *Sandinista Now!* would undoubtedly mislead the listener due to the high production value across the twelve tracks included. Though it doesn't have the sheen and precision of Sandy Pearlman's production on *Give 'Em Enough Rope* (1978), the new style spearheaded by Mick Jones is much more ambitious compared to the raw intensity of their debut or the comparatively streamlined mixing on *London Calling*.

One difficult thing about this experiment is that we know all thirty-six tracks from *Sandinista!* exist. Admittedly, one could critique this methodology of choosing this as the template on the basis that it may not be the *best* twelve tracks on the album. Nevertheless, these are twelve tracks that CBS and Epic devised as being an easy access point for the master work. And no matter the twelve, one will always have the knowledge of the other twenty-four and argue, *but what about this one? What about that one?* Before that is discussed, it is necessary to take a close look at the songs that make up *Sandinista Now!*

3
Side One

Police on My Back

While *Sandinista!* famously opens with the hip-hop number "The Magnificent Seven," the condensed twelve-track version of the album, made to highlight the album's commercial potential, opens with a cover done in a more predictable Clash style. The Clash were no strangers to covers and have many throughout their catalog. Their first album contains the band's iconic take on Junior Murvin's "Police & Thieves," the first of many reggae numbers in their discography. Their 1979 *Cost of Living* EP opens with a cover of "I Fought the Law," originally written by Buddy Holly and The Crickets' guitarist Sonny Curtis. Both covers indicate two important Clash characteristics: the affinity for Black musical traditions and their empathy for those on the "wrong side of the law." Such factors make "Police on My Back" by The Equals an obvious choice for a Clash cover.

The Equals were one of England's first integrated rock bands in the 1960s whose guitarist and primary songwriter was Guyanese-British musician Eddy Grant. Famous for his 1983 hit "Electric Avenue," Grant was born in British

Guiana, a colony on the northern coast of South America. In 1953, People's Progressive Party leader Cheddi Jagan was democratically elected as prime minister of the colony and was soon overthrown by the British government who believed Jagan was a communist paving the way for the Soviet Union in South America. By the time Guyana achieved independence in 1966, a more conservative government led by Forbes Burnham had been in power with the support of the United States. In 1980, the Marxist and Pan-Africanist scholar Walter Rodney, who had compared Burnham to Somoza in Nicaragua, was assassinated. It is widely believed that Burnham was involved in plotting the assassination. To what extent The Clash were aware of any of these connections between Grant and Guyana, Forbes and Somoza, and the assassination that happened only six months prior to the album's release is unknown. Regardless, contextualizing the original song, its writer, and his birthplace undoubtedly unlocks a deeper understanding of the song and justifies it as a thematically appropriate album opener.

Like The Clash's first single "White Riot," "Police on My Back" starts with a siren sound. While the band's early single uses actual audio of a police siren, the more sophisticated Clash that play on *Sandinista!* create the siren with guitars, staying true to The Equals' original. Still, they couldn't resist inserting the sound of a getaway train halfway through the song. The alarming sound of the guitars and the steady drumbeat make for an exciting opener, but what makes The Clash version rise above The Equals is Mick Jones' cry, "What have I done?" during the bridge. Jones takes what's essentially a spoken-word moment in the original recording and turns it into an impassioned melody worthy of being released as a single. It may be worth mentioning that "Police on My Back" was also the first song recorded for *Sandinista!* at Power Station studios in New York, and therefore may have set the tone for what was to come.

Somebody Got Murdered

A notable feature of the *Sandinista Now!* promo is that it has back-to-back tracks led by Jones at the top of the album. It's not surprising since Jones' "Train in Vain" peaked at number 23 on Billboard's Hot 100 in the States. In fact, half of the songs on side one of *Sandinista Now!* have Jones at the lead instead of Strummer, but "Somebody Got Murdered" exemplifies the strengths that Strummer and Jones each bring to the table. Recorded in Wessex, the song was originally meant to be used for the soundtrack to William Friedkin's 1980 crime thriller, *Cruising*, starring Al Pacino. Music producer Jack Nitzsche called Strummer requesting a "heavy rock number." Strummer came up with the idea for the song after a parking attendant was murdered at the World's End housing estate where he was living at the time over a matter of five British pounds. According to Strummer, "That night I wrote the lyric, gave it to Mick and he wrote the tune. We recorded it and Jack Nitzsche never called back."[1] Perhaps Nitzsche was expecting something with Strummer's voice in mind instead of Jones' nearly whispery vocals. It's also likely that Nitzsche wasn't expecting to get something as compassionate or empathetic as a lyric like "I've been very hungry, but not enough to kill" to be used in a movie about a cop going undercover to catch a serial killer targeting gay men with Pacino's likeness. Whatever the reason, "Somebody Got Murdered" is a fine example of Strummer's ability to write about issues where violence and poverty intersect, and Jones' ability to turn those sentiments into melodic rock numbers.

The Call Up

During the summer of 1980, President Jimmy Carter issued Presidential Proclamation 4771, reinstating the Selective Service System for all men born on or after January 1, 1960. According to Jones, "the registration for the draft affected a lot of our fans in America. I remember going to a demonstration on the Upper West Side."[2] The response to this outcry is the first single released for *Sandinista!* "The Call Up" starts with a primitive drum machine, another siren, and a Marine chant before kicking off with a funky groove, xylophones, and a lethargic Joe Strummer. Sean Egan describes the song as "more poetic lament than rallying call."[3] The lack of ferocity in Strummer's tone doesn't seem to reflect the anger felt by their American fans who were outraged over a potential draft, calling into question whose perspective he's singing from.

Strummer sings, "it's up to you not to heed the call up, I don't want to die." Clearly, it is up to young American men to be conscientious objectors, but who is the "I" Strummer is referring to? To be sure, he isn't concerned that *he* would personally be the victim of the American military in the event of war. Additionally, it doesn't seem like "I don't want to die" and "I don't want to kill" are from the American perspective, no matter how true it may be for anti-war Clash fans. Instead, Strummer appears to be singing from the perspective of a potential victim of increased American military presence around the world. The character Strummer has created is fearful, not angry. He's another young man who still has places to see ("I want to see the wheatfields over Kiev and down to the sea") and wants to fall in love ("There is a rose that I want to live for . . . There is a dance, and I should be with her") yet he fears for his life. The song has a tragic ending when the Marine march is heard once more as Strummer pleads, "I don't want to die." This was lost on listeners who heard the song for the first time by seeing the music video of The Clash donning a confusing array of military attire, following a dissolve from an image of a letter with the heading "On Her Majesty's Service" despite conscription not being a threat to young men in England.

Washington Bullets

If there is anything positively gained from the *Sandinista Now!* tracklist, it's that "Washington Bullets" is no longer buried twenty-three tracks deep. As the closest thing to a title track, "Washington Bullets" is arguably the most essential song on the album. Not only because it's the only song to mention the Sandinistas, but because it's Strummer's attempt at a punk rock jeremiad, backed by the band embracing music well outside their punk roots. Furthermore, the song encapsulates who The Clash are and what they stand for. Opening with an enormous drum fill that is followed by Topper Headon on the marimba, "Washington Bullets" is The Clash's take on calypso music. Strummer has assumed the role of the *griot*, a lead singer who serves as storyteller, poet, and historian in West African and Afro-Caribbean traditions. On "Washington Bullets," Strummer and The Clash adopt this call-and-response tradition to edify the listener about state violence primarily perpetrated by the United States in Jamaica, Chile, Cuba, and Nicaragua.

First, Strummer focuses on Jamaica: "the cocaine guns of Jamdown town / the killing clowns / the blood money men / are shooting those Washington bullets again." Like Guyana, Jamaica was a British colony until they were granted independence in the 1960s. After achieving independence, Jamaica was run by the conservative Jamaica Labor Party (JLP), until 1972 when democratic socialist Michael Manley of the People's National Party (PNP) served as prime minister until 1980. Between the general election of 1976 and the following election in 1980, gang violence in Jamaica intensified. It was during this time that Manley was being challenged by the JLP candidate Edward Seaga, otherwise known as "CIAGA" because of his affiliations and support from the CIA who supplied gangs connected to the JLP with weapons. Those same gangs, such as the Shower Posse, were also notorious for trafficking cocaine. No one was safe from the threat of violence during these election cycles.

Jamaica's 1976 general election was held on December 15, just ten days after the Smile Jamaica concert and twelve days after Bob Marley was shot for headlining the event. Despite one of the core Rastafarian values of being categorically against all "isms," Marley's involvement with the Smile Jamaica concert was perceived as an endorsement for Manley, and it is widely believed that Seaga and the JLP are responsible for the attempted murder of Marley in his own home, days before the concert and election took place. Famously, Marley refused to be intimidated by violence and went on with the performance. However, after the concert, he exiled himself in England where he recorded both *Exodus* and *Kaya* in 1977. It is during these sessions when Marley recorded "Punky Reggae Party." Marley didn't return to Jamaica again until 1978 for yet another concert that propelled him to mythic status.

In 1978, Bob Marley and the Wailers headlined the One Love Peace Concert that was organized by two rival gang members who shared a prison cell together during a brief truce period. Claude Massop and Aston Marshall's idea for the concert was to unite Jamaica for what was referred to as the Third World Woodstock. Against all odds, both Manley and Seaga were in attendance. Aware of this, Marley called both politicians to the stage during his set. With the rivals on either side of him, Marley had Manley and Seaga joined hands at center stage while Marley said a prayer and continued to play. The symbolic joining of hands was an ecstatic concert viewing experience, but the realities surrounding the moment were much darker. Unbeknownst to Marley, the sound equipment for the concert was used to smuggle guns into the country from the United States, and by 1980, when Seaga became the prime minister, 889 people would be murdered in the span of a year, including organizers Massop and Marshall.[4]

As longtime admirers of reggae music, The Clash had tried and failed twice to write and record on the island. In preparation for their sophomore album, *Give 'Em Enough Rope*, Strummer and Jones had gone to Jamaica for ten days before returning to England with only a couple of songs written. Strummer said, "we were in full punk regalia . . . me and Mick had no idea about anything."[5] Though they were fans of reggae and the cult film *The Harder They Come*, the English pair hadn't considered the turbulent conditions of post-colonial Jamaica. Chief among the songs written while staying in Kingston was "Safe European Home," which chronicles their trip with Strummer singing, "I went to the place where every white face is an invitation to robbery / and sitting here in my safe European home / don't wanna go back there again." Egan explains, "the track expresses thankfulness for being back in comparatively tranquil Blighty and a simultaneous self-disgust at that relief."[6] Despite the disenchanted lyric, the band did go back again in 1980 with Mikey Dread to record material for *Sandinista!* However, violence had intensified since their last visit, and they fled for safety at the request of Dread. In "Safe European Home," Strummer is eager to geographically distance himself from Jamaica seemingly for fear of petty theft. However, a more enlightened Strummer appears on "Washington Bullets" to contextualize what he has witnessed firsthand and expressed his realizations about US involvement in Jamaica's tumultuous election year.

The next verse deals with Chile. Before changing his name to Joe Strummer, John Mellor went by the name Woody after the folk icon Woody Guthrie. In addition to Guthrie, one of the folk heroes to greatly influence Strummer was Chilean artist and activist Victor Jara, who was a key part of the New Song Movement consisting of folk musicians dedicated to the socialist ideals promoted by Chilean president Salvador Allende, who was elected in 1970 as part of the Unidad Popular (UP) coalition consisting of Chile's various left-wing parties. However, on September 11, 1973, general Augusto Pinochet staged a coup with the support of the CIA. Gunshots and explosions could be heard when Allende gave his final speech over the radio before taking his own life. Strummer urges his listeners, "remember Allende and the days before / before the army came." In this instance, Strummer wants to remind his audience of the hope and reality of leftist revolutions in the modern era. On the other hand, he urges those listening to "please remember Victor Jara in the Santiago stadium."

The morning following the coup, Jara and thousands of others who were affiliated with Allende were gathered and taken to Chile Stadium. Being a famous musician who had campaigned for Allende, Jara was recognized and subsequently tortured. Members of Pinochet's military junta broke the guitarist's hands and wrists, yet Jara continued to sing the protest songs, namely "Venceremos" which translates to "We Will Win." Jara died a martyr's death in the Santiago stadium when he was shot in the head, followed by countless rounds of machine gun fire. His corpse was then displayed outside the stadium before being discarded in a mass grave. "Es verdad," sings Strummer. It is true, and it's because of Washington bullets. Backed by the United States,

Pinochet and his junta government ruled as a dictatorship in Chile until his death in 1990. And it wasn't until forty years later that anyone was charged for these acts of state-sponsored terrorism. Therefore, as Strummer contends, it is important to remember martyrs like Jara. Even though Strummer himself would not live to see it happen.

Moving on to Cuba, "Washington Bullets" switches its tone. In 1952, Cuban presidential candidate Fulgencio Batista staged a coup three months before the election. With no chance of winning, Batista seized power with the support of the Cuban military, forcing President Carlos Prio Socarras into exile and ruling as a military dictator. Once again, Batista's rise to power was recognized and backed by the United States. However, on July 26, 1953, armed revolutionaries led by Fidel Castro attacked the Moncada Barracks, sparking the beginning of the Cuban Revolution. The revolution continued until 1959 when Cuba's Communist Party gained control over the country and severed ties to the United States.

"And in the Bay of Pigs in 1961 / Havana fought the playboy in the Cuban sun," recounts Strummer. Originally devised by the previous Eisenhower administration, the newly elected John F. Kennedy followed through with an attempt to overthrow Castro with CIA-trained Cuban exiles who were provided with American planes painted to resemble those of the Cuban air force. Coincidentally, the planes took off from pre-revolutionary Nicaragua. Between April 17 and April 20, the Washington bullets were no match against Cuba due the clumsy and inefficient execution of the CIA-sponsored Brigade 2506. To be sure, America's inability to overthrow such a small country was an international embarrassment.

On the other hand, it made Cuba and Castro appear even stronger than the world had previously perceived them. In the decades that followed, Castro became one of the main villains in America's Cold War mythmaking.

Following the verse about Cuba, the album's central chant is finally heard, as backing vocalist Ellen Foley and others cheerfully exclaim "Sandinista!" Whereas Strummer's retelling of the Jamaican and Chilean tragedies is sung with a sense of defeat ("es verdad"), the Cuban verse ends victoriously and exuding hope ("Sandinista!"), leading the listener into the verse dedicated to the titular Nicaraguan revolutionaries. The Sandinistas named themselves after the rebel Augusto César Sandino, who declared war against the United States and their occupation of Nicaragua from 1927 to 1933. Through the efforts of guerilla warfare with combatants who were typically indigenous, working-class people, Sandino fought against the US Marines as well as Nicaragua's own National Guard led by Anastasio Somoza Garcia, which was created with the intent of stabilizing the country after the U.S. withdrew from the country. The United States began removing troops from the area following the 1932 election and had officially left in 1933 as part of President Franklin D. Roosevelt's Good Neighbor Policy opposing government interference in Latin America. A year later, Somoza and the National Guard had Sandino killed, and his remains have never officially been identified. By 1936, Somoza forced President Juan Bautista Sacasa to resign and assumed power until his assassination in 1956.

Following the death of Anastasio Somoza Garcia, his sons continued to lead the country. Anastasio Somoza Debayle took office from 1967 and 1972. The West Point graduate was also the head of the Nicaraguan National Guard and served as a de facto leader of the country even when he left office in 1972. However, Somoza returned to office in 1974. His strongman leadership style and endless grabs at power following a natural disaster created humanitarian crises for the people of Nicaragua. During this time, the Sandinistas were able to grow and gather more support as the people turned against the Somoza dynasty.

Taking their name from Sandino, the Sandinista National Liberation Front (FSLN) was originally formed by Carlos Fonseca, Silvio Mayorga, and Tomás Borge in the 1960s as a small group of students and other young activists who embraced a grassroots approach. As they gained support in the late 1960s and into the 1970s, they initiated guerrilla-style attacks with limited success, and their lack of preparation forced them to reevaluate their tactics by first continuing to strengthen the organization. After the deaths of Fonseca and Mayorga, the FSLN were split into three factions, or tendencies. The Prolong Popular War (Guerra Popular Prolongada) emphasized rural guerilla warfare like that of their namesake. Similarly, the Proletarian Tendency centered on Marxism and urban mobilization. The "Third Way" led by brothers Daniel and Humberto Ortega, known as the Terceristas, advocated for a coalition of anti-Somoza groups outside the FSLN to expand the fight and lead an insurrection. The three factions reunited by 1979 and successfully overthrew Somoza in a matter of months.

Strummer sings, "For the very first time ever when they had a revolution in Nicaragua / there was no interference from America / Human rights in America / The people fought the leader and up he flew / With no Washington bullets what else could he do?" The United States had been a strong ally for Somoza. During the conflict, the United States tried to negotiate with Somoza to ameliorate human rights issues in Nicaragua as well as prevent the FSLN from seizing power. Somoza's refusal to concede led to the United States to terminate their financial support for Somoza and Nicaragua. Without the support of the United States, the FSLN were able to successfully overthrow Somoza and his National Guard, and the Carter administration, perhaps surprisingly, directed aid to the newly formed Sandinista government based on human rights initiatives.

Though the Soviet Union supported Cuba and Nicaragua, The Clash still criticized the Cold War superpower when addressing the Soviet-Afghan War. Additionally, Strummer sings, "Ask the Dali Lama in the hills of Tibet / 'How many monks did the Chinese get?'" in reference to the Chinese invasion and annexation of Tibet. The Dali Lama was forced to flee Tibet in 1959 and has lived in exile in India ever since. It may seem contrary for a band to celebrate the achievements of other Marxists while criticizing both the USSR and China, but The Clash very clearly objected to imperialism on either side of the Cold War. In the song's final verse, The Clash reflect on their own country's sins: "In a war-torn swamp, stop any mercenary and check the British bullets in his armory." The punk rock choir continues to cry out "Sandinista!" over the joyous sounds of the marimba to celebrate the potential for young, progressive revolutions throughout the world. For as much Cold War paranoia and threat of destruction that occurs on the record, "Washington Bullets" ultimately serves as the centerpiece and thesis of the record. It is a record that wants to be optimistic about the 1980s thanks to the example modeled by the FSLN.

Ivan Meets G.I. Joe

During an interview with *Rolling Stone* in April 1980, Mick Jones was asked if he would go to war if Britain reinstated the draft, to which Jones responded, "That's out of the question. This is an important fact: people prefer to dance than to fight wars. In these days, when everybody's fighting, mostly for stupid reasons, people forget that. If there's anything we can do, it's to get them dancing again."[7] The Clash believed in music as a tool to promote a message of anti-violence, and though they were sometimes criticized for not offering solutions to the issues they sang about, Jones posits that encouraging people to dance and providing the music is itself a solution. On "Ivan Meets G.I. Joe," The Clash pushed this idea to its most absurd potential by imagining the Cold War as an epic dance battle.

As celebrated as Topper Headon's contributions as a drummer are for *London Calling*, and even *Give 'Em Enough Rope*, much of what's been written about him during the *Sandinista!* sessions concern his struggle with addiction. While that's true, Headon's multi-instrumental abilities shine throughout the record. In the case of "Ivan Meets G.I. Joe," he plays all the instruments. The same is true for *Combat Rock*'s "Rock the Casbah" which became a major hit for The Clash after Headon was kicked out of the band. However, "Ivan Meets G.I. Joe" is the only Clash song that features Headon as the main vocalist. That said, his vocals are nearly buried by the post-disco, early hip-hop cacophony that gives the impression of Headon as the real-time commentator at the name-checked Studio 54 or Le Palace.

"Ivan Meets G.I. Joe" found admirers in scholars Samuel Cohen and James Peacock who write, "it provides a clear demonstration of how experimental, sophisticated and inclusive The Clash's music became during their five-year career as a four piece . . . it offers a musical transnational vision as complex as anything the band recorded."[8] In addition to the overt farce of the scene and darkly comedic dance moves, ranging from the "Cossack Spin" to the "Vostok Bomb," Cohen and Peacock add an additional interpretive layer of comic deflation by likening the track to the British nursery rhyme "Orange and Lemons," indicating the childish antics of the world powers.[9] They take their analysis one step further and suggest that the song may even be about internal Clash struggles with the titular "Joe" representing American G.I.s, Joseph Stalin, and Joe Strummer. No matter the artists' intention, the song is a unique moment in the band's catalog that captures The Clash at their most creative and absurdist.

Hitsville U.K.

No matter how free they felt to create a genre-defying triple LP, The Clash were still battling their label to have it released. In fact, The Clash had fought and won battles with CBS for the entirety of their career. Famously, the label released "Remote Control" as a single to support their eponymous debut album. In return, The Clash slyly released "Complete Control" as retaliation. Their greatest pre-*Sandinista!* victory against CBS was to have the *London Calling* double LP sold for the price of one by telling them the second disc would be a bonus 12" single. To be sure, these battles with their label gave The Clash some rebellious credibility and allowed them to maintain their integrity as a punk act. It was especially important for The Clash's own mythology to have such fights since the decision to sign with a major label was considered by punks to be the very death of England's punk movement. Strummer, on the other hand, justified the move based on the label's distribution, which maximized their ability to spread their message across the world. Nevertheless, the seemingly contradictory act of the anti-establishment band being a product for the major label was something some fans couldn't reconcile, a burden felt by the band throughout their career. Nowhere is this more apparent than on *Sandinista Now*'s side one closer, "Hitsville U.K."

Originally released as one of the singles for *Sandinista!*, "Hitsville U.K." is a Motown-inspired number that also pays respects to the growing indie rock scene in the UK. Named after Motown Records' headquarters in Detroit, Hitsville U.S.A., Jones continues where he left off with the success of "Train in Vain." While "Train in Vain" effectively convinced listeners that it was a cover of an actual R&B song by successfully adopting the style and language of classic tunes like Ben E. King's "Stand by Me," "Hitsville U.K." fails to capture the essence of Barry Gordy's hit factory in its sound or lyrical content. In the song, Jones duets with his then girlfriend, Ellen Foley, who back in 1977 appeared on Meat Loaf's *Bat Out of Hell*, where she triumphantly displayed her vocal prowess on the lengthy and operatic "Paradise by the Dashboard Light." None of these elements seem to be relevant or compatible with The Clash sound, and that must be the point. In fact, there isn't much of a link between Motown and the rapidly growing indie labels in the UK apart from their emphasis on the importance of producing 7" singles.

On the track, the duo name-checks the burgeoning indie labels in the punk and new wave scenes in Britain. Jones admires the efforts of London's Small Wonder (The Cure, Bauhaus), Edinburgh's Fast Product (Gang of Four, The Human League), West London's Rough Trade (Cabaret Voltaire, Stiff Little Fingers), and Manchester's Factory Records (Joy Division, New Order), commending artists who bypassed "slimy deals with smarmy eels" with nothing but a mic and boom in their living rooms. Each of these labels and their artists dared to embrace a DIY ethos to achieve success on their own terms without dependence or intervention from major labels. By 1980, it looked like the goals of punk were being realized by a new generation who witnessed the so-called selling out of some of the movement's pioneers. Jones expresses his regrets as a major label artist by celebrating the rise of new wave on a track that is admittedly a poor choice for a single, regardless of the sentiment.

4
Side Two

Up in Heaven (Not Only Here)

One of the defining characteristics of The Clash's early identity was their association with life in London's tower blocks. So much so that *NME*'s Tony Parsons referred to The Clash sound as "Towerblock Rock"[1]—a nod to Bob Marley's own brand of "Trenchtown Rock." In the 1960s, the aging urban housing structures that had barely survived the passage of time and the not-so-distant Second World War were demolished and replaced with new high-rises to accommodate the post-war generation. According to Egan, amenities such as indoor bathrooms, central heating, and the novelty of the new towers were appreciated for a short period, but the tower block lifestyle was, in a word, soulless. Furthermore, the design of the estates themselves were grim and categorized as "New Brutalism" in terms of style.[2] The lack of pride, as Egan notes, led to vandalism, setting the stage for rugged punk aesthetics in the following decade.

"Up in Heaven" completes a trilogy of songs in The Clash catalog about Jones growing up with his grandmother in

Wilmcote House that starts with "London's Burning" from their debut album, followed by "Lost in the Supermarket" from *London Calling*. Like "Lost in the Supermarket," Jones takes the lead to great effect. Singing with a confidence that's lacking in "Hitsville U.K.," he describes urine-soaked elevators, graffiti as proof of life, and domestic disputes between hate-filled wives and their unaffected husbands. Strummer's poetic and social realistic lyrics here are elevated by Jones' ability to turn them into a groovy musical arrangement with melodies that make the track an album standout. Jones sings "You can't live in a home which should not have been built / By the bourgeois clerks who bear no guilt / When the wind hits this building this building tilts / One day it will surely fall to the ground." What risks being poignant yet clunky lyrically works masterfully with Jones' pop sensibility, especially as his echoey, reverbed vocals intensify and then fade as if falling from atop the tower block. The most tragic event involving the tower blocks that happened while members of The Clash were coming of age was the gas explosion at Ronan Point in 1968 that left four dead. As recent as 2017, however, a fire at the Grenfell Tower killed seventy-two people and injured dozens more.

What makes "Up in Heaven" a unique Clash track is that Strummer also borrows lyrics from a deep cut from folk singer Phil Ochs titled "United Fruit." Jones sings, "it has been said not only here," before singing the Ochs section: "Allianza dollars are spent / To raise the towerin' buildings / For the weary bones of the workers / To be strong in the morning." In the spirit of the album, The Clash are not examining their own experience as something wholly unique but as a shared experience with Latin American countries. Like "Washington Bullets," Ochs' song recounts the United Fruit Company, the Banana Wars, and the US military intervention in these countries. The Clash's comparison is imperfect, if not slightly problematic. To be sure, Ochs' song about the evils of neocolonialism and the rise of America as a new superpower that exploits the land and people of Latin America doesn't compare to the woes of Brutalist architecture. According to Cohen, however, this attempt to connect "the distant to the close at hand" is what makes The Clash a transnational phenomenon.[3]

The Magnificent Seven

One of The Clash's early quintessential tracks was the abrasive and affective "I'm So Bored with the U.S.A." from their self-titled album. The song served as an anthem for British punks' distaste for American politics and pop culture. By *London Calling*, however, their adoration for American R&B, rockabilly, and the Wall of Sound were on full display. America's influence went a giant step further when they decided to work on *Sandinista!* in New York at Electric Lady Studios. Like *London Calling*, *Sandinista!* has songs that are an homage to American popular music of the 1950s and 1960s. However, the band had also become infatuated with New York's then-burgeoning hip-hop scene. Most enamored was Mick Jones, who spent his time in the big city walking around with a giant boombox, commonly referred to as a "ghetto blaster." Jones had even acquired the nickname

"Whack Attack" due to fascination and absorption of this new style that could be heard all over the city's streets.

Despite having its first commercial hit in late 1979 with the Sugarhill Gang's "Rapper's Delight," hip-hop was still far from the mainstream. Until the Sugarhill Gang, hip-hop's recorded history was slim to none, yet the scene was expanding at an accelerated rate in clubs and local radio stations that were becoming obsessed with this post-funk, post-disco sound. For British listeners, the sound may have reminded them of the toasting done by reggae and dub artists like Clash collaborator Mikey Dread. While the Sugarhill Gang had the first commercially released hip-hop record, the group was far from being the most celebrated act within the scene itself. Groups like The Cold Crush Brothers, The Treacherous Three, Funky 4 + 1, and Grandmaster Flash and The Furious Five dominated the underground scene. As witnesses to this growing genre, The Clash's embrace came in the form of "The Magnificent Seven."

The title fit in well with all the number-based groups dominating the scene, but it's also a reference to the 1960 John Sturges western of the same name, which is itself a reimagining of Akira Kurosawa's 1954 masterpiece, *Seven Samurai*. In Kurosawa's film, the noble samurai's swords are no match for the muskets they face when protecting a desperate village—a cautionary tale for musicians who failed to adapt to the ever-changing musical landscapes of the late 1970s into the following decade. For The Clash at least, Sturges' *The Magnificent Seven* undoubtedly was the more influential of the two films. In the movie, a rag-tag group of gunslingers are assembled to protect a vulnerable village from bandits. After the final showdown, the gunslingers face a devastating loss and realize that only the farmers won—an appropriate metaphor for a band who would put everything they had into a triple album only to forgo their royalties so that the fans would be guaranteed three LPs at an affordable cost.

Most importantly, the title refers to waking up at 7:00 a.m. for a seven-hour workday (plus an additional hour to "do your thang"). Over the five and a half minutes, Strummer sings about the monotony of working-class labor, the pressures to provide, police violence, and alcoholism, while name-dropping Socrates and Plato, President Nixon, Gandhi and MLK, and Marx and Engels. The hip-hop cadence along with its emphasis on clever and comical rhymes allows Strummer to show off his abilities as a writer and singer beyond punk's limitations. To be sure, he is much more successful at "rapping" than Debbie Harry on Blondie's "Rapture" and David Byrne's brief "facts" rap on Talking Heads' "Crosseyed and Painless." Strummer's interest in politics and the plight of the working class also gave hip-hop its first overtly political record, predating Grandmaster Flash and Furious Five's "The Message" that was released in 1982. Besides, when Bill Stephney approached Chuck D about the concept of Public Enemy, the idea was for the groundbreaking group to be the hip-hop equivalent to The Clash, not CBGB's more popular adopters of the new sound. Likewise, the Beastie Boys have cited The Clash as being an essential influence during their early hardcore punk era in the early 1980s and equally important later in their career on groundbreaking albums like *Check Your Head* (1992), *Ill Communication* (1994) and

Hello Nasty (1998) that are similarly noted for their genre diversity. Furthermore, the riff from "Straight to Hell" on *Combat Rock* is now commonly recognized as the sample for M.I.A.'s mega hit "Paper Planes."

The Clash did not simply write a novelty hip-hop song to hitch their proverbial wagon to the growing trend. More than being consumers and adopters of hip-hop music, they actively supported the New York scene. During their iconic run of concerts at Bond International Casino in 1981, not only did they invite punk bands like Dead Kennedys and The Fall to open, but they also used their platform to introduce their audiences to The Sugarhill Gang, Grandmaster Flash, and The Treacherous Three. Unfortunately, many people in their audience were not receptive to the hip-hop acts. The post-disco sound of old school rap likely enraged the rock music fans whose motto had become "disco sucks" after the notorious Disco Demolition Night at Comiskey Park in Chicago only two years earlier, where thousands of outraged rock lovers set fire to disco records and other LPs from Black and queer artists. Actor Steve Buscemi, who co-stars with Strummer in Jim Jarmusch's *Mystery Train* (1989), was at a Bond show and witnessed the audience's backlash toward Grandmaster Flash. According to Buscemi, Strummer reprimanded the crowd for booing and not giving them a chance, urging them to *really* listen.[4]

The song opens *Sandinista!* and is curiously booted to the second track on side two of *Sandinista Now!* Consequently, Strummer's quip "fuckin' long innit?" is a solid joke for a long opening track for a thirty-six-track album that is lost on the listeners bound to this single LP version. Though the song doesn't appear to have much in common musically or thematically with any of the previous tracks, it is essential for understanding The Clash's belief in embracing new music and the culture that fosters the new sound. Jones' post-Clash group, Big Audio Dynamite, allowed him to continue exploring this new sound. Also, there may have been a missed opportunity on the sixth side of the record to include Jones' "Magnificent Dance" remix that was successful on New York's hip-hop radio stations.[5]

The Leader

The longest song on *Sandinista Now!* is followed by the shortest track on either version of the album, finishing after a hasty 1:41 minutes, compared to "The Magnificent Seven's" 5:28 minute runtime. Unlike the evolving hip-hop exploration before it, "The Leader" looks back to rock's rockabilly beginnings. With their quiffs and rolled up sleeves, it's no mystery as to how The Clash would wind up recording a rockabilly number. In the early 1980s, there was a rockabilly revival that emerged alongside punk rock in both the United States and the United Kingdom. The CBGB scene had Robert Gordon, whose first two albums in the late 1970s were collaborations with rock guitar pioneer Link Wray. Gordon's sound and the songs he was recording were more than homage or pastiche. The attempt seems to convince listeners that they had unearthed something from a bygone era. On the other hand, The Cramps had their own approach to rock's most primitive genre, creating an entirely new subgenre of "psychobilly." Produced in Memphis, Tennessee by Big Star legend Alex Chilton, *Songs the Lord Taught Us* (1980) captures the sound of rockabilly while evoking images of the B-horror pictures of the 1950s, namely *I Was a Teenage Werewolf*. Across the Atlantic, Welsh rockabilly revivalist Shakin' Stevens and his band The Sunsets were immensely popular among England's Teddy Boys who were first generation rock 'n' roll conservatives. Teddy Boys and their offspring who were prone to violence and were known to fight provocative punks whose "kill your idols" mantra threatened the Teds in the early years of British punk.[6] By 1980, however, even Queen had a rockabilly pastiche on the radio with "Crazy Little Thing Called Love." A year later, The Stray Cats released their first album and quickly became the most successful of the retro-rock acts. The Clash, as one might imagine, had a different approach to rockabilly.

"The Leader" kicks off with a guitar riff and shuffling snare drum reminiscent of Carl Perkins or Eddie Cochran. Strummer even uses inflections and a cadence that are trademarks of rockabilly singing style, but the production style is enough to offend genre purists. Its most notable departure from the rockabilly of old is the lyrical content. Strummer sings about a topic so notorious and scandalous that it has been adapted into a film, a musical, and television series, and he condenses it into a fast-paced rockabilly number with no shortage of exposition despite its chorus being a singular lyric "the people must have something good to read on a Sunday." The subject, of course, is the infamous Profumo Affair. The Clash's titular leader is Secretary of State for War under Prime Minister Harold Macmillan, John

Profumo. Other characters include a Russian spy named Yevgeny Ivanov, osteopath and socialite Stephen Ward, and the so-called femme fatale Christine Keeler.

A dancer and friend of Ward's, Keeler had sexual relations with both Ivanov and Profumo, and—along with many other young women and British elite during the sexual revolution of the 1960s—attended orgies complete with a nude "masked man" rumored to be an aristocrat who was whipped by attendees. This gives multiple meanings to the words "the leader never leaves his door ajar / he swings a whip from Boer War." On one hand, the leader could be "swinging" with a "whip" as in having an affair with a political figure who is meant to ensure party members are voting in accordance with their values. Strummer's recontextualization of these figures makes even their titles sound akin to BDSM. On the other hand, the leader could be swinging a whip acquired from the South African War to erotically punish the masked man. Strummer's mention of the Boer War keeps this song that sounds like it's being read straight from the tabloids connected to the themes of imperialism and colonialism captured throughout the album. Reimagining these spoils of war being used for elitist orgies is one of Strummer's most comic and scathing indictments of the ruling class.

The "fat man" with "Vodka fumes" refers to Ivanov, while the "thin man" refers to Profumo, both of whom "touch her," that is Keeler. The fat man/thin man dichotomy is also a popular trope in comedies from the vaudeville stages to the movie screens. Recasting Ivanov and Profumo as the fat man and thin man reimagines these political figures as Laurel and Hardy style goofballs. The subtextual punchline is that Profumo lied to the House of Commons about his affair and later resigned after an investigation found otherwise. Furthermore, Prime Minister Macmillan also resigned because the scandal had successfully discredited the conservative government, allowing the Labour Party to come to power in the following election. While not a typical protest song, Strummer and The Clash are having a laugh at the lingering Victorian ideals losing their strength because of a revolution not overtly political, but certainly sexual.

Junco Partner

The second cover song on the single LP edition of *Sandinista!* is the New Orleans R&B staple "Junco Partner." The song was already in rotation in setlists for Joe Strummer's previous pub rock band, The 101ers, and he would continue to play it late into his career with his post-Clash band, The Mescaleros. It's safe to assume that Strummer had some sort of affinity for the junkie character or at least the junkie subgenre. The song is also the one track The Clash were able to successfully record with Mikey Dread at Studio One in Jamaica before the band fled the island due to the violent threat of "drug men" approaching the studio. One of the great marks against The Clash and the album is the lack of credit given to Mikey Dread, although he still spoke highly of them up to the end of his life. But no song has a more complicated history with credits on the album than "Junco Partner."

The song has been covered by everyone from Dr. John, Professor Longhair, James Booker, and even Harry Connick

Jr. Additionally, the song is a riff on the blues number "Junker's Blues" and has inspired other songs like Chuck Berry's similar yet goofy track "The Man and the Donkey." The first and most popular version of the song, however, is the 1951 recording by James Wayne, produced by the grandfather of filmmaker Judd Apatow, Bob Shad, who was eventually given credit for the song. Dr. John, who covers the song on 1972's *Dr. John's Gumbo* notes in the liner notes that while Wayne popularized the song, it was "the anthem of dopers, the whores, the pimps, the cons . . . the song they sang in Angola, the state prison farm, and the rhythm was even known as the 'jailbird beat.'" Regardless, The Clash initially credited James Booker on the first UK release of the triple LP. The Clash covered a diverse range of artists during their short career, but perhaps none were more eccentric than Booker. Known as the "Black Liberace," the one-eyed, queer piano player was known for wearing an eyepatch with silver star on it, which he can be seen sporting on the cover of his 1976 album, *Junco Partner*. While the Wayne version from 1951 has an early R&B feel that sounds like a precursor to rock 'n' roll, Booker's version is twice as long and grooves out with adlibs that match the vibe of The Clash's own reggae rendition of the tune. There may be few people who would count "Junco Partner" as one of the twelve essential tracks from *Sandinista!*, but perhaps there was some intention behind the second half of *Sandinista Now!* featuring the tracks most rooted in the American South: the rockabilly "The Leader," the blues number turned reggae (and eventually dub) take on "Junco Partner," and the gospel finale "The Sound of Sinners."

One More Time

Despite not being represented on any of the post-career Clash compilations, "One More Time" captures something about *Sandinista!* that felt essential enough to include on *Sandinista Now!* The most recognizable feature is its reggae groove. Though plenty of Clash tracks utilize reggae rhythms, what sets "One More Time" apart is the obvious influence of Mikey Dread as a co-producer of the track. The track contains all of Mick Jones' reverb heavy riffs while being polished by the more experienced of the two producers, Dread himself. Dread's involvement elevates the track that is repetitive both musically and lyrically. Strummer's melody is a standard reggae cadence that plays out without Strummer putting on a voice like he has on "Junco Partner." And like all good reggae and Clash songs, it is political in nature. One of the most interesting moments in the song contains a reference to the Watts riots that occurred in Los Angeles in 1965 and the Freedom Riders who passed through Montgomery, Alabama in 1961.

Regarding Watts, Strummer predicts the 1992 Los Angeles riots following the Rodney King verdict when he sings "watch when Watts town burns again / the bus goes to Montgomery." Curiously, Strummer refers to Montgomery rather than the incident in Anniston in which a bomb was thrown in the Greyhound bus carrying the Freedom Riders. Photos of the bus in flames became one of the most important and iconic images of the civil rights movement. Perhaps these references feel familiar to Strummer and The Clash since Wattstown ("Watts town") and Montgomery are both locations in the UK. Neither have experienced a violent civil rights movement analogous to the United States, but the message of The Clash has always been that such a movement is possible. If it can happen in "Watts town," it can happen in Wattstown.

The Sound of Sinners

Before they decided to name their third album *London Calling*, the band had considered the title "The Last Testament." The idea was to repurpose the first rock 'n' roll album cover with Simonon's bass striking down, opposed to Elvis' ascending acoustic guitar. Similarly, an alternate title for *Sandinista!* was "The Bible," possibly because of the volume of the triple LP.[7] Even though John Lennon's remarks about The Beatles being bigger than Jesus created an outrage that caused many in the United States to boycott the Fab Four, especially in the South, the most provocative and offensive title the UK punks could ascribe to their 1980 album would be a reference to radical socialists rather than a statement misunderstood as sacrilege. Undoubtedly, "The Sound of Sinners" would automatically be a better closer for an album titled "The Bible," but its inclusion even on a single LP version of *Sandinista!* offers genre diversity that makes the record such a landmark.

Four years before David found the chord that pleased the Lord in Leonard Cohen's "Hallelujah," Strummer was searching for the "jazz note" that brought down the Walls of Jericho. According to the Hebrew scriptures, God told Joshua to circle the Walls of Jericho for seven days with priests armed with horns, bringing down the walls so that the Israelites could kill every man, woman, and child, as well as their livestock. For Strummer, this served as a biblical analogy for The Clash and their punk cohorts: "they blew the horns and the walls of the city crumbled . . . Well, punk rock was like that."[8] Ultimately, it further demonstrates Strummer's belief in music's ability to change the world. Complete with Tymon Dogg on the organ and Den Hegarty from the doo-wop revival group Darts as the spoken-word evangelist, the content of the song is anti-gospel while also highlighting complicated truths about religious faith.

In the much-repeated chorus, Strummer sings, "after all this time / to believe in Jesus / after all those drugs / I thought I was him." He's referring to a phenomenon in which people on drugs come to believe that they are Jesus Christ. Yet it also calls to mind a similar mental phenomenon commonly referred to as the Jerusalem syndrome. For decades, there have been instances of tourists, sometimes with little-to-no history of mental illness, who arrive in Jerusalem and become convinced that they are the Christ. Even though these cases involve people who take hallucinogenic drugs or experience brief or long-term psychosis, the everyday reality is that religious believers habitually form Christ in their own image.

For some believers, Jesus stands for supposed traditional family values and represents homophobic ideals. For others, he's a radical leftist whose acts of charity ought to be reflected in policymaking rather than oppressive discriminatory laws. Even Biblical scholars and theologians debate the Christology of Jesus of Nazareth by emphasizing either his humanity or divinity. Frankly, the gospel writers of the New Testament are split on this debate. Surprisingly, the end of the chorus reaches a genuine gospel conclusion that Strummer sings sincerely as he portrays the role of the punk reverend: "I ain't good enough / I ain't clean enough to be him." Of course, reggae is also very religious music, and early rock music and its forefathers were gospel singers who combined the sacred with the profane, so it isn't entirely far-fetched that The Clash would eventually adopt the sound of the pious and sinners alike.

If one is willing to entertain *Sandinista Now!* as an appropriate single LP alternative to the original triple LP, then one thing it has to offer is a strong side one. Beginning with the cover of "Police on My Back," by The Equals—a racially integrated British group with roots in Guyana whose political struggle mirrors events for the titular Sandinistas—and followed by "Somebody Got Murdered," the rejected song for the *Cruising* soundtrack, is fitting start for an album title that references the Nicaraguan rebels and a classic American war film. Getting to the heart and soul of the album, it's safe to say that no condensed version of *Sandinista!* would work as well without the conscientious objector anthem "The Call Up" and the quintessential Strummer takedown of imperialism and dictatorships that is "Washington Bullets." "Ivan Meets G.I. Joe" also fits well with the political themes, but, equally important, it provides the one and only song in The Clash's catalog sung by Topper Headon. While "Hitsville U.K." strays from the message of state-sponsored violence and foreign politics, it comments on The Clash's mythology, their contradictions, and their support for artists who were able to succeed without succumbing to the stigma of selling out by signing with a major label.

Side two of *Sandinista Now!* is a greater indicator of the eclectic nature of its main source. The side two opener "Up in Heaven (Not Only Here)" is one of Jones' career highlights with The Clash that covers tower block life in England while lifting the words of American protest singer Phil Ochs to connect the band's own experiences to those in Latin America. It's followed by their first attempt at adopting hip-hop, "The Magnificent Seven," which they continue to do on *Combat Rock* and Jones pursues in his post-Clash band Big Audio Dynamite. Finally, the politically charged sex comedy disguised as a rockabilly number about the Profumo scandal ("The Leader"), a reggae-punk hybrid reimagining of the New Orleans rhythm and blues classic ("Junco Partner"), the Mikey Dread collaboration ("One More Time"), and—of all things—a gospel tune that is a personal favorite of Elvis Costello's ("The Sound of Sinners") make for incredible side two that touches on British and American culture. To be sure, *Sandinista Now!* is a solid LP with a tight set of songs held together by shared themes and a variety of genres—but is it better than *Sandinista*?

Part II
Sandinista!

Sandinista Now! only scratches the surface of what The Clash wanted to do musically. Not only does this single-disc version of the record not have all the dub tracks that people typically criticize but it also misses some of the most impressive and beloved songs ever written by Jones and Strummer. Therefore, the following chapters will examine the remaining twenty-four tracks from the three LPs to determine if more was lost than gained when dramatically cutting the list of songs produced by The Clash for *Sandinista!*

Disc one has five songs that aren't on the promo, which fill in a lot of exciting musical gaps. There's a waltz in 3/4 time, a cover from jazz and blues pianist Mose Allison, bassist Paul Simonon's only contribution as a singer on the album, and the dub version of "One More Time" with Mikey Dread's trademark toasting. Disc two features more songs that break from the punk mold, including more reggae-inspired tracks, another rockabilly number, and the punk equivalent of improvised jazz, "Broadway." Additionally, the song "If Music Could Talk" opens a conversation about the recording of *Sandinista!* in New York's Electric Lady Studios, complete with a designated spliff bunker, a variety of guest musicians, and far-out genre experimentation. The third LP is the only one to not have any songs represented on the *Sandinista Now!* promo. Curiously, the first track is hardly a Clash song at all. The following track, "Charlie Don't Surf," was a recommended track from the *Gavin Report* that missed the promo cut despite being a reference to *Apocalypse Now*. A Clash favorite, "The Street Parade" is an informal closer to the most accessible songs on the album before using "Version City" as an introduction to side six where, according to Strummer, "only the brave go." The album finishes with three dub tracks, a small group of children singing The Clash's 1977 song "Career Opportunities," and finally a slower instrumental piece, "Shepherds Delight," which ends in a cacophony of sound that manifests the message written in the matrix across all six sides of vinyl: "IN SPACE . . . NO ONE . . . CAN . . . HEAR . . . YOU . . . CLASH!"—a reference to the tagline for Ridley Scott's *Alien* (1979). Rather than dedicating chapters to each side of vinyl, the following chapters will be divided by the three discs to determine the merits of the classics, deep cuts, and filler that make up the triple LP.

5
Disc One

Something About England

There's only one song from the first side of *Sandinista!* that didn't make it on the *Sandinista Now!* promo. While the other songs are Clash takes on hip-hop, R&B, reggae, disco, and rockabilly, "Something About England" goes to even less expected territory by appropriating the sounds of late nineteenth and early twentieth century music hall numbers. With "asthmatic, Salvation Army brass and tinkling piano,"[1] as Pat Gilbert puts it in his Clash biography, *Passion is a Fashion*, the song is a dream-like number involving two characters that move through time to reshape the protagonist's understanding of his home country. Jones' character opens the track by reporting on elitist concerns and fears about immigration, petty theft, and fear for the decline of genteel English society. Strummer's vocals are soon introduced as he portrays the character of an old man who will teach the young Englishman a lesson in Dickensian fashion. The old man explains that he was abandoned by his family during the First World War and suffered through the hunger strikes during the depression while "the ladies lifted cake to their mouths." Strummer's old man then fought in the Second World War, witnessing the deaths of millions.

What follows is a response to "It's a Long Way to Tipperary." Even more so than "Junco Partner," the song has a complicated publishing history, as there are numerous writers, singers, and publishers credited with its authorship. However, it's best known for being a popular marching song during the First World War. It can be heard everywhere, from Jean Renoir's anti-war masterpiece *La Grande Illusion* (1937) to Charles Schulz's *Peanuts* cartoons. Even the Ramones have their own take with "It's a Long Way Back to Germany." The song is about an Irish soldier marching through England, saying farewell to Piccadilly and Leicester Square, as well as to his beloved Molly-O. Because of the song's popularity, it became associated with the valiancy and dignity of service men. Decades later, Strummer revisits the song from the perspective of someone who has since come back from the war with a new perspective, free from romanticization. Strummer sings only "the few returned to Piccadilly / We limped around Leicester Square." Here Strummer subtly emphasizes that most soldiers never returned home and those who did came back injured. Finally, Strummer's mythical character leaves Jones warning him to "remember the tales I tell" as a ghostly choir of dead soldiers can be heard singing their old marching song. Since the rest of side one is mostly inspired by American music, there was little chance this track would make it on a condensed promo copy of the record for American DJs with the hope of getting it on the radio. It is unmistakably English in its sound, message, and poetic sense of structure. It's also one of the most unique and interesting tracks found on any Clash album.

Rebel Waltz

Side two begins with another strange venture for The Clash that is a worthy follow up to "Something About England" yet a bizarre move for a punk band. True to its title, "Rebel Waltz" features a 3/4 time signature accompanied by horns and harpsichord. It takes well over a minute before we hear Strummer's vocals. Instead, there is a slow build of guitar, bells, horns, and harpsichord, and an enormous snare sound. When all the instruments finally come together, Strummer's voice joins in a manner unlike listeners have heard him before. He isn't angry. He almost sounds like he lacks any passion, relative to his previous work. His subdued vocals set a tone for a new kind of Clash song that breaks from Strummer's typical social realism and into something surreal. The dream-like quality of the music is realized lyrically when Strummer sings "I slept as I dreamed of a long time ago / I saw an army of rebels dancin' on air," only to immediately follow it with "I dreamed as I slept" of the rebels waltzing on air.

Next, Strummer becomes one of the soldiers dancing with a girl to a song that was meant to be "danced in the battlefield." He hears a voice saying "stand 'til we fall," perhaps meaning party 'til we drop. Suddenly, news breaks that this war is not yet ended, and the soldiers must return to the battlefield believing that "the war could not be won." Now in battle, Strummer and the rest of the soldiers are dancing with rifles to the rhythm of gun fire—an image like "Ivan Meets G.I. Joe," but instead of being a dark comedy with a disco groove, "Rebel Waltz" uses irony and surrealism to express a humanist's perspectives on war. Finally, Strummer hears "stand 'til you fall," shifting from the plural to the singular. It recalls the rebel waltz and dancing with the girl, but here the phrase has been perverted. The order is now coming from a commanding officer telling the soldier to be brave in the battlefield and face death. Or it could be the case that the soldier has been captured by the enemy and is now receiving orders from a firing squad.

There's no shortage of interpretive moves to be made with "Rebel Waltz," as it is one of Strummer's most poetic attempts at songwriting. It's exceptionally effective since Strummer never has to raise his voice to get his point across. Instead, there's a rare gentleness to his voice that guides the listener through the song, calling special attention to the lyrics, not as a rallying call, but as something more contemplative. Notably, the song doesn't make specific reference to any conflict from the past or present. The vagueness of the events in terms of geography allows the listener to imagine themselves in any time, in any place, during any conflict, just as Strummer does as he sleeps while dreaming of a rebel waltz transcending the dance floor and battlefield. Tracks like "Something About England" and "Rebel Waltz" are distinctly from this era of The Clash's output and are, therefore, essential in understanding what makes *Sandinista!* an endearing record worthy of the 3LP format.

Look Here

Mose Allison was a blues and jazz pianist, singer-songwriter from the Deep South who moved to New York during the beatnik 1950s. He's been covered by The Who, Leon Russell, Van Morrison, and Elvis Costello. The Pixies even have a song named after Allison on their 1990 album *Bossanova.* Allison's combination of blues and jazz music makes it easy to understand how he would inspire acts like The Who and Van Morrison, but The Clash, or any British punk band, kept their distance from the blues rock that dominated the 1960s British rock scene. Nevertheless, The Clash added Allison to their growing list of artists to cover, not to mention adding jazz to their list of genres to tackle with punk rock tenacity. As a matter of fact, the cover was done on the insistence of Topper Headon, whose frenetic drumming gives the low-key jazz number a punk rock transformation. The other musicians, who aren't even Clash members, made the track what it is. The song features Lew Lewis from Eddie and The Hot Rods on harmonica, Mickey Gallagher on the keys, and Norman Watt-Roy on the bass. Gallagher and Watt-Roy from The Blockheads guest all over *Sandinista!* and offer a set of skills on "Look Here" that truly wouldn't be possible without their talents.

The lyrics don't seem to have any political connotations, but the upbeat cover The Clash and company create taps into the urgency in Allison's words. While others might croon over the jazzy rhythms, this gang of vocalists chant "What ya think you're gonna be doin' next year / How you know you're not gonna up and die? / Soon enough your friends with find you out / You might not have enough time to spare." Then the instruments take off like a shotgun blast. It's paranoiac, insecure, and fearful, yet above all else playful. It's hard not to apply these words to Headon's status in The Clash as his addiction to heroin became increasingly self-destructive. *Would he still be in the band next year? Is death right around the corner?* Headon may not have known it at the time but "Look Here" seems to be an attempt to exercise his demons or flee from them at breakneck speed.

The Crooked Beat

Paul Simonon's first contribution as a singer for The Clash is "The Guns of Brixton" on *London Calling*. It's a reggae number with a groovy bassline and an iconic Clash hook for a chorus. Even though Simonon was gone for a lot of the making of *Sandinista!* to shoot the movie *Ladies and Gentlemen, The Fabulous Stains* (1982), he still managed to get a track of his own on the album. As the band's most reggae-obsessed member, it follows that Simonon would turn in a reggae and dub number for the record. Unlike "Guns of Brixton," Simonon is the writer of the song, despite *Sandinista!* being the first Clash record to give the songwriting credits to the band.

Admittedly, there is an amateurism to the songwriting. It can be heard in Simonon's voice as he emphasizes each syllable on "mid-night run," "South Lon-don," "the bass, gui-tar, and drums." But instead of being about a violent encounter inspired by *The Harder They Come* (1972), "Crooked Beat" is an earnest song about Simonon's love for the genre and his experiences of going to parties to hear that crooked, crooked beat. Simonon and others are seeking out the latest hi-fi sound to dance off the pressures of everyday life with guitar, bass, drums, a cymbal splash, and a word of truth. For Simonon and other attendees, these parties are liberating, cathartic, and edifying. At the same time, however, there's a threat of police violence. He sings "cars patrol this crooked beat / badges flash and sirens wail / they'll be takin' one and all to jail," emphasizing that the street is not being patrolled, but rather the sound itself and the culture it produces. As an outsider looking in, he doesn't say *we'll* be taken to jail, which subtly comments on the racist police forces and acknowledges his own privilege. The second half of the song is essentially a dub mix of the first half with Dread's trademark toasting finishing off the track and segueing into "Somebody Got Murdered." While it's far from the best song on the album, part of what makes *Sandinista!* unique is that it's the only album of theirs to feature a song from all four members, and for that reason "The Crooked Beat" is indispensable.

One More Dub

The final track on disc one is nobody's favorite and feels weird to discuss without its predecessor, but "One More Dub" is, if anything, the earliest foreshadowing of what's to come on the final side of the triple album. It's basically a reprise of "One More Time" with more of Dread's toasting, and its sole function is to extend the groove. It's an odd thing to hear a song five tracks into an album then immediately follow it up with what might be a throwaway B-side for a single release, but one can find the humor in Dread starting the song by saying "stop wasting time!" It's a long way to "Version City."

6
Disc Two

Lightning Strikes (Not Once but Twice)

The influence of hip-hop strikes not once but twice on *Sandinista!* "Lightning Strikes" is similar to "The Magnificent Seven" in a few ways: Headon's drums, the length of the track, and most obviously, Strummer's rhymes. However, Strummer's rhymes aren't as interesting, playful, or skillful as they are in the previous track. Look no further than "if this is spring then it's time to sing / never mind the little birdie's wing." What we get at the start of the second LP isn't a fun hip-hop track as much as a stream of consciousness about Strummer's experiences in New York, of which there will be more to come. That isn't to say that the song isn't packed with ideas and references that remain faithful to the numerous themes and motifs in the album.

The song starts with a radio broadcast from New York City's WBAI, a progressive and independent station that has been on the air since the 1960s, when it earned a reputation for hosting anti-Vietnam War activists, feminists, comedians, avant-garde music, readings from novelists and poets, and so forth. In 1980, a Marxist from the Caribbean named Samori

Marksman became a programmer who could be heard that summer interviewing fellow activists like Angela Davis. While The Clash were known to cover songs from artists that they want their fans to be aware of and to use their shows to introduce their audiences to artists they revered, "Lightning Strikes" is a rare occasion of them turning people onto a radio station, specifically one that is a useful source for hearing news reports from the progressive left.

The first verse is Strummer's attempt to capture the rapid energy of the city when lightning strikes in Old New York. The second verse comes off as more critical at the mention of the city's one and only tree that can be found in Garbage Park, then warns not to visit it after dark. Verse three is what listeners may expect from The Clash. In this instance, the strike is a reference to the NYC transit strike in 1980. Strummer sings, "accidental hike in the transit strike / roller skate or ride a bike / three to a car, Brooklyn Bridge / you won't get far with your privilege." It's not the most enthusiastic endorsement of the transit workers' strike, but he does offer practical solutions for those opposed to the transit strike. One might expect Strummer to weigh in a bit more, but he immediately jumps to his struggle to decipher the graffiti that he admires regardless of not being able to read it. The punk from London Town continues to explore what else New York has to offer.

Strummer strolls through Harlem and is able to score pot cheaper than the price of booze in the Bowery. There's no reference to any of the artists from the Harlem Renaissance, but there aren't any references to the past at all. "Lightning Strikes" is only concerned with the present, and the song functions as a cultural travelog. Next, lightning strikes in the form of a Polaroid flash, presumably near the historic Stonewall Inn: "Caught in the act / you're married too and that's a fact / but I won't peek, and I won't squeak / Down by the trucks on Christopher Street." Again, there's no mention of the Stonewall riots and the gay liberation movement that it spawned. Strummer is more concerned with spotting a married man in a part of the city known for its queer culture in the act of a homosexual affair.

Strummer has witnessed the cityscape, the transit strike, Black culture, and queer culture. Before the song finishes, he manages to fit in Cuban, Jewish, and Chinese cultures with a quick "it's Cuban Day, oy vey! / Chinese New Year, let's call it a day." Later he hears a Puerto Rican melody, then sings "'Hey Chi-man' is what he's speaking." Pat Gilbert notes this as a racial moment,[1] perhaps because of the previous reference to the Chinese. Unfortunately, it's also possible that it is a reference to "chi chi," the patois slur for a gay man. One would hope this is another instance of Strummer just reporting what he's heard in the streets, which in this case would either be overtly homophobic or racist. The song never reaches the heights of "The Magnificent Seven" and has some missed opportunities as well as some questionable if not outright regrettable moments no matter how true to 1980s New York.

Corner Soul

The earliest version of The Beatles hit "Get Back" was a protest song that included lyrics like "don't need no Puerto

Ricans," "don't dig no Pakistanis," "you'd better get back to your Commonwealth homes." This improvised satire from Paul was in response to conservative parliament member Enoch Powell. In 1968, Powell gave his infamous "River of Blood" speech on immigration. Referencing Virgil's *Aeneid*, Powell expressed fear and paranoia over the growing immigrant population in England and feared that mass violence would lead to rivers of blood. Notting Hill Carnival is the second-largest Afro-Caribbean celebration in the world and the largest in Europe. In "Corner Soul," Strummer opens with a chorus about the music of Carnival and asks, "is this music calling for a river of blood?" According to the verse that follows, this is not a personal concern of Strummer's. The question is coming from those within "the big meeting" who are preparing to declare war on Ladbroke Grove.

The rhetorical question over whether the "music" is calling for a river of blood is a euphemism for Black people and culture. It's easy to imagine white conservatives fearing for their lives upon hearing Bob Marley sing about killing cops ("I Shot the Sheriff") and feeling like he wants to bomb a church ("Talkin' Blues"). Since the 1980s, conservatives have been blaming rap music as a cause for violence. Attacking the music of Black cultures is a roundabout way to espouse racist rhetoric while trying to maintain plausible deniability. To be sure, that rhetoric coming from the top-down creates tension between the state and people of color.

In the verses of "Corner Soul," the people must be warned about the threat of violence. Ladbroke Grove is only ever referred to as the Grove, exoticizing the scenario.

The response to the outcome of the big meeting has these characters weighing their options: “Does it mean I should take my machete to chop my way through the path of life? / Does it mean I should run with the dog pack?” The song is incredibly dark and dramatically displays how tension is created between the government and the populace. On the other hand, it’s one of Strummer’s best performances on the album. His empathy and compassion manifest in his inflections, in contrast to his angrier performances on early Clash albums. Here, Strummer is a passionate mediator backed by Ellen Foley and accented by Headon’s snare and cymbal that emphasize every word.

Let’s Go Crazy

When the darkness of “Corner Soul” ends, the celebratory “Let’s Go Crazy” shortly follows. Beginning with a clip of reggae artist Ansell Collins calling for peace at the Notting Hill Carnival, the song erupts into a Caribbean soca that is The Clash’s best and most successful effort to capture the sound of Carnival in the studio. Nowhere on the album is Headon more impressive as a marimba player and his own drum circle. Strummer’s vocals give the impression of an entire crowd singing and chanting over symbolic victories like the sinking of a White Star Line shipping vessel at the dock, a metaphor for the decline of the British Empire. Though the drums heard are being played by Headon, Strummer mentions a Rastafarian drumming away 400 years of dread—a reference to The Wailer’s own “400 Years” about colonialism, slavery, and exile, as foretold in Genesis 15 according to the Rastafarian belief. The Rasta equivalent to gospel music, Nyabinghi rhythm, is important to reggae music because it is meant to be a collaborative effort consisting of improvised syncopation and call-and-response drumming with religious chants. Additionally, the famous Trinidadian Calypso singer Mighty Sparrow is name-checked.

While the music is joyous, the lyrics take yet another turn to bring attention to the threat of violence committed by the police. You can go crazy, but you still have to "be careful" and "watch yourself" because the "lawful force" is here and backed with the "indiscriminate power of arrest." Strummer refers to "sus laws" rooted in the Vagrancy Act of 1824. Sus laws are stop-and-frisk laws that British police can use on any suspicious person. In its earliest applications, it was used against the poor, sex workers, and men caught in engaging in sexual acts. With the rise of immigration, people of color became a primary target. According to the Institute of Race Relations (IRR) in the UK, "Scrap Sus" movements began in the late 1970s. The Black People's Organisations Campaign Against Sus coalition and others "forced the issue onto the government's agenda, and by 1980 the Select Committee on Home Affairs would recommend immediate repeal, which was achieved in 1981."[2] However, the 1981 Criminal Attempts Act that repealed sus was replaced with the Police and Criminal Evidence Act (PACE) in 1984 and expanded in the Criminal Justice and Public Order Act in 1994. By 1999, the Terrorism Act intensified sus laws despite being deemed a human rights violation and is still being implemented today.[3] These temporary victories and perpetual defeats are why the Carnival is an essential space for self-expression. Yet even there, racist law enforcement looms heavily over the event. Despite the potential threat of state-sponsored violence, the celebration continues, and the message of joy and peace on Earth today rather than in some distant afterlife is preached in the song's conclusion.

If Music Could Talk

There's a quote attributed to French New Wave director Jacques Rivette that claims, "every film is a documentary of its own making." Perhaps the same can be said about music. It may literally be the case on "If Music Could Talk." This stream of consciousness experiment in stereo features two different ad-libbed vocal tracks panned on each side, respectively, against a smooth reggae groove. Naturally, there's an instant reference to Joe Strummer's spliff bunker, as if to say "it seemed like a good idea at the time." Over the course of the song, Strummer is waiting for Clash opening act Bo Diddley, announces that Frank is on the phone, discusses Errol Flynn's legacy with Headon, quotes Elvis, praises touring mate Joe Ely, mentions Buddy Holly and The Crickets, and admits to feeling lonely standing on the floor of Electric Lady Studios. Lastly, Strummer confesses, "I'm just wasting a great big corporation the entire fund . . . I'm wasting the whole thing." Despite the banality, the reggae groove, piano, and constant saxophone solo against Strummer's competing vocals in both stereo channels make for a fun listen and prove that the "anything goes" spirit of this record can pay off in unexpected ways.

Midnight Log

Unlike "Look Here," "Midnight Log" is a rockabilly track that sounds less like a revival and more akin to what might have been heard twenty-five years prior. Lyrically, however, it isn't as straightforward as "Look Here." The moral of the story appears to be: in the end, the devil comes to collect, whether you're a crooked accountant or a cop. However, the second verse seems entirely unrelated to the premise, as if Strummer has stumbled into Travis Bickle's apartment in Martin Scorsese's *Taxi Driver* (1976): "Worried for my friend as he shows me round the flat . . . He don't believe my speech that lines can and should be drawn / like if he had a shotgun the barrels would be sawn." The song becomes much more interesting in its final verse when Strummer turns inward: "I don't believe in books, but I read them all the time / for ciphers to the riddles and the reasons to the rhymes." Strummer appears to be questioning his persona as the well-read punk who is expected to have answers to questions about Marx, foreign policy, civil and human rights issues, violence, and more. He's searching for the answers to these problems in books and finding solutions he doesn't fully subscribe to. Worse, he's looking for a meaning not only for his songs, but for his own existence. The titular midnight log could be the devil keeping track of his debtors, the books for the accountants and cops in cahoots with the devil, or the late-night ramblings of Strummer burdened with existential dread.

The Equaliser

Sandinista! is generally critiqued for its excessive dub tracks, especially those buried on the sixth side of the album. However, "The Equaliser" is The Clash and Dread offering up the best dub track they ever collaborated on. It's the moment The Clash go from being a band that covers and imitates reggae and dub music to having their own definitive style. Flourishes like the eerie sound of Tymon Dogg's violin give the track a flourish that sets it apart from not only other Clash tracks, but other dub and reggae artists. At 5:46 minutes, it's one of the longest songs on the album, and it doesn't have the up-tempo drums and bass of "The Magnificent Seven" to guide listeners through the track with the ease of a pop song. Instead, listeners have to sway through a dense cloud of sonic pot smoke. Even though it's long, by no means does it overstay its welcome. Strummer repeatedly sings "We don't want no gangboss / We want to equalize." According to Strummer, labor in industrialized England has been joyless and debilitating. While "The Magnificent Seven" details the mundaneness of the average workday and how it withers the soul, other songs where the self-professed socialists appear to discourage manual labor altogether.

In "Clampdown" from *London Calling*, Jones sings "the men at the factory are old and cunning / you don't owe nothin,' boy get running! / it's the best years of your life they want to steal." The subtextual message of early Clash songs like "Clampdown" is that factory jobs are not the only option. The Clash were famously one of the hardest working bands in the punk scene who were constantly playing, writing, rehearsing, touring, recording, and releasing new material. For them, creating music and pursuing art is labor intensive and energy not to be wasted in an assembly line. Still these early Clash songs risk looking down on people who have been duped into the factories and settle for being functioning cogs who knowingly contribute to a system that exploits them. With only a few years behind them, "The Equaliser" is more sympathetic and reaches out to laborers rather than punching down. Strummer sings "'til half and half is equalized, oh put down the tools . . . see the world you have built with shoulders of iron / see the world, but it is not yours, say the stealers of Zion." Adopting the language of Rastafarians, Strummer encourages laborers to strike until they're awarded equal pay. They're no longer the old men in the factory who have wasted their lives, but dignified members of the working class who should stand up for their rights in solidarity. Like "Washington Bullets" and "The Call Up," "The Equaliser" is an essential track that demonstrates the spirit of *Sandinista!*

Broadway

Whereas the old man in "Something About England" details life in England from the so-called Great War through the depression and aftermath of the Second World War, set to a nineteenth-century British musical hall number, "Broadway" requires a uniquely American genre. The free-spirited jazz instrumentation and its title that calls to mind one of America's other great cultural exports, the Broadway musical. Strummer assumes the role of a homeless man and tells his story while the talents of Headon and Gallagher are on full display, demonstrating once more their ability to cross genres with great ease and mastery. Yet Strummer is not out-performed here. His coolness in the verses, with his mumbled crooning and impassioned vocals as the music rises, is one of the best examples of Strummer learning how to use his voice as an instrument. In the booklet for the *Clash on Broadway* boxset, Clash roadie Garry "The Baker" Barker explains that the persona Strummer is adopting is a homeless man outside of the Algonquin Hotel sleeping on a heating vent who Strummer used to watch intently.[4]

Strummer imagines this man as a tragic American figure from American cinema, a former boxer who was born during the depression, who unlike Brando's Terry Malloy in *On the Waterfront* (1954), probably never even had a shot at being a prizefighter. "Born into misery," the man has been knocked around in the ring and in life. The old man says, "oh, the loneliness / used to knock me out harder than the rest." He goes on about how he wants a car with a full tank of gas to greenlight his dream to get out of the city. Instead of lecturing about poverty in the United States and damning the social system that allows for a growing homeless population in the streets of post-Vietnam New York, Strummer uses a more humanist approach by attempting to understand the man by characterizing his experiences and desires. For some, this is one of the greatest achievements of *Sandinista!* And then—apropos of nothing—the song fades out, only to come back with Gallagher playing piano for his young daughter who sings parts of "Guns of Brixton"—a song that has nothing to do with "Broadway" geographically, tonally, musically, generically, racially, generationally, or lyrically. For many, this is one of the most baffling moments on *Sandinista!* and perhaps The Clash's catalog.

7
Disc Three

Lose This Skin

What better way to start the final disc of a triple LP than with someone else's song? Tymon Dogg is a longtime friend of Strummer's from the early 1970s. As a multi-instrumentalist, Dogg had the reputation of being a prodigy and a mentor to Strummer, who was still going by the name Woody when they met.[1] In fact, it was his days accompanying Dogg, while busking in the streets playing Chuck Berry covers, where Strummer first earned his chops.[2] The two then played together in Strummer's pre-Clash band, The 101ers, and later reunited in The Mescaleros. With Dogg playing such an important part in Strummer's musical origin story, it's fitting that he would give Dogg the opportunity to announce himself on such an epic record. According to Gilbert, Dogg considered the inclusion of his song as a "gesture of largesse," remembering, "The Clash worked on that track for days of their own recording time . . . There was a real openness and generosity of spirit at that time . . . It felt like they'd got this facility now and they really wanted to share it. They didn't have to do that."[3] For those confused by this level of inclusivity, the final verse reflects their criticism of the album: "What's it like to be so free? / So free it looks like lost to me."

Charlie Don't Surf

Even though *Sandinista Now!* is a reference to Coppola's *Apocalypse Now*, and "Charlie Don't Surf" is even mentioned as a recommended track, it is absent from the promo LP. The title and hook come directly from a line in the film uttered by Robert Duvall, playing the aptly named Lt. Col. Kilgore. It opens and closes with the psychedelic sounds of a helicopter propeller that resembles the movie's groundbreaking sound design. According to Strummer, "Film was a big part of our cultural life. Somehow film seemed more important at the time."[4] The time that Strummer is referring to is the rise of New Hollywood cinema in the late 1960s through the 1970s. A Clash favorite was Martin Scorsese, who was a mutual fan of The Clash and owned an imported copy of the original debut album. Production photos from the set of *Raging Bull* (1980) reveal Scorsese wearing Clash T-shirts. One can even spot The Clash as extras in his 1981 cult classic *The King of Comedy*.

The New Hollywood filmmakers arrived after the decline of the studio system and the oppressive Hays Codes, granting them greater creative freedom. This new class of young filmmakers, who grew up on classic Hollywood and New Wave cinema from around the world, utilized and adopted the best of both worlds and rejected the stifling conservatism of Old Hollywood to redefine American cinema. Their movies reflected the violence of everyday life, the Vietnam era, and the sexual revolution while challenging political and cultural norms similar to British and American punks who laid the groundwork for New Wave music. As these filmmakers became more successful, their ambitions grew larger. The production of *Apocalypse Now* has become a mythic tale of obsessive auteur-driven cinema going too far, but the success of the film, for better or worse, proved that Coppola's self-destructive set was justified.

For *Sandinista!* fans, the film is a fitting analogy for the sprawling masterwork. For others, *Sandinista!* is The Clash's *Heaven's Gate* (1980). While the production disasters of *Apocalypse Now* resulted in one of Hollywood's most beloved works of cinema, Michael Cimino's *Heaven's Gate* was just the opposite. Similarly burdened with troubling stories from set and bad press, the epic western with a running time over 3.5 hours long is generally regarded as the movie that put an end to large-scale epics from auteur directors of the New Hollywood era. *Heaven's Gate* lost so much money that the studios lost confidence in movies and filmmakers of a similar ilk. In the case of The Clash, they continued to pursue political themes, especially concerning Vietnam, on *Combat Rock*, which includes the song "Red Angel Dragnet" featuring a spoken-word section with Clash consigliere (a term borrowed from *The Godfather*) Kosmo Vinyl, who recites one of Travis Bickle's monologues from Scorsese's *Taxi Driver* (1976). Despite appearing to follow in the thematic footsteps of the American auteurs of the 1970s, The Clash did scale back what would have been a double LP down to a single record for *Combat Rock* to intentionally avoid another *Sandinista!*

Nods to cinema aside, the song is packed with references to American popular culture to satirize its legacy of imperialism in the twentieth century. Insisting that Charlie, a sort of nickname for the Viet Cong, ought to catch waves over a surf rock style guitar and vocal melody is an ironic suggestion that the Vietnamese communists need to adopt an American lifestyle. In this case, a laid-back California lifestyle. In the first verse, Strummer and Jones adopt the perspective of American soldiers singing, "We've been told to keep the strangers out / We don't like them starting to hang around / We don't like them all over town / Across the world we're going to blow them down." With a cadence reminiscent of 1960s bubblegum pop, The Clash critique America's prejudice toward immigrants and the violent proxy wars around the globe during the height of the Cold War. The song is equal parts clever, humorous, and even bleak like the best songs from Elvis Costello & The Attractions' biting satire on *Armed Forces* (1979). An additional fun fact: Tears for Fears lifted the line "everybody wants to rule the world" for their 1985 classic of the same name that became a number one hit.

Mensforth Hill

In *Apocalypse Now*, the characters are sent on a special mission down river. The further down the river they go, the trippier the movie gets. The same can be said for *Sandinista!*, especially in the case of "Mensforth Hill," which functions as

The Clash's own "Revolution 9." The track revisits "Something About England," but instead of Dread simply toasting over the track, they play the song in reverse. Generally regarded as filler, perhaps there's something beautiful about this moment when one considers the song they've chosen to reverse and how it could recontextualize the track. "Something About England" is mostly about an old man who recounts his time growing up in England during the First World War, the depression, the hunger strikes, fighting in the Second World War, and the aftermath of living with the devastation of wartime. What if reversing the song is a poetic attempt to musically evoke a moment in Kurt Vonnegut's classic anti-war novel *Slaughterhouse-Five*?

In the book, the main character Billy Pilgrim is a Second-World-War-veteran (and surrogate for Vonnegut himself) who was present at the bombing of Dresden and becomes unstuck in time. Consequently, he winds up watching a war film forward and backward. By replaying the movie in reverse, Vonnegut describes fires magically being extinguished, shards of metal being sucked into the bellies of planes, and bullets and scraps of metal being removed from peoples' bodies. The bombs are then taken back to the factories where people worked day and night to dismantle the munitions, as specialists cleverly hid the minerals used to make these weapons "so they would never hurt anybody ever again."[5] Whether this is the intended meaning of "Mensforth Hill" is irrelevant. The track's obtuse structure allows for such a reading to be imposed on it. One can choose to hear the song as nonsensical filler or to consider Vonnegut's vision of a war in reverse that is consistent with themes of the album.

Junkie Slip

Britain's precursor to rock 'n' roll music came in the form of skiffle. With folk origins, it was easy to learn, easy to play, and typically upbeat, making it easy for young musicians to pick up quickly and form a group. "Junkie Slip" is essentially a skiffle-junkie tune that's upbeat, bouncy, and even sounds funny due to Strummer's hiccupping vocal delivery throughout the song. Though the band protected Headon from the media when it came to word about his heroin use, it's hard not to think of this song as a condemnation. It's the album's second junkie number and the third pre-rock 'n' roll track to "Look Here" and "Midnight Log." It doesn't offer much apart from being a much-needed buffer between the experimental "Mensforth Hill" and the more straightforward rock number that follows.

Kingston Advice

Revisiting the theme of violence in Jamaica, "Kingston Advice" may be one of the most underrated songs on the album. It's a big rock song filled with sound effects and echoey call-and-response-style vocals that make it one of the most interesting production efforts on *Sandinista!* It's also a great indicator of where the band is going sonically with *Combat Rock*, specifically "Inoculated City." Like "Washington Bullets," the song covers the rise in gun violence in Jamaica, where young people have easier access to firearms than they do food, and calls out the government as the source of both direct and indirect forms of violence. In the end, Strummer is overwhelmed: "In these days, I don't know what to do / The more I see, the more I'm destitute . . . I don't know what to sing / The more I know, the less my tune can swing." If Strummer is feeling fatigued about the reality of violence, political unrest, and his responsibility to comment on it by side five of the record, the listener likely feels similarly. Yet this track stands out as an underappreciated gem that may have received more affection if not for its placement on the third LP.

The Street Parade

The inclusion of "The Street Parade" as a hidden track on the *Clash On Broadway* box set may be more significant than its role as a side five closer of *Sandinista!*, but it demonstrates that there was something important or even quintessential about the song. Drums play while a delayed guitar rings out in a separate tempo. A sound like a laser beam from a B-picture follows and continues spontaneously. Staccato steel drums attempt to make sense of rhythm. Strummer arrives once again sounding defeated, lonely, and desperate, but without disguising it with a genre diversion: "When I was waiting for your phone call / The one that never come / Like a man about to burst / I was dying of thirst." A saxophone responds with a similar melody supported by rolling steel drums building to a boisterous guitar that cuts through the track in direct opposition to Headon's standard 4/4 rhythm. Competing with the discord, Strummer's voice rises defiantly: "I will never fade." Alone, Strummer is self-defeating, yet he refuses to "get lost in this daze." His solution is to "disappear and join the street parade." To understand what sounds like a contradictory sentiment, Ernst Fischer explains that humankind's ultimate desires are communal:

> Evidently man wants to be more than just himself . . . He is not satisfied with being a separate individual . . . He rebels against having to consume himself within the confines of his own life . . . He wants to refer to something that is more than "I," something outside himself and yet essential to himself. He longs to absorb the surrounding world and make it his own; to extend his inquisitive, world-hungry "I" in science and technology as far as the remotest constellations and as deep as the innermost secrets of the atom; to unite his limited "I" in art with communal existence; to make his individuality *social*.[6]

Strummer never disappeared from pop culture even after the demise of The Clash. He acted, scored movies, collaborated with Mick Jones on Big Audio Dynamite, released solo albums, and created what is lovingly called Strummerville at the Glastonbury music festival. Starting in 1995, Strummer formed a campsite at the fest that grew into a twenty-four-hour campfire for those in the know to lounge, listen to music, and commune together. Since Strummer's death, Strummerville has become an official part of Glastonbury, complete with its own stage. According to filmmaker Julien Temple, Strummer once told him that his legacy may be his campfires.[7] Today, Strummerville is also associated with the Joe Strummer Foundation, a charity dedicated to supporting projects around the world that create empowerment through music. To be sure, "The Street Parade" has taken on a new meaning since Strummer's death, but for true fans of *Sanidinista!* it has always secretly been one of The Clash's best songs.

Version City

Before The Clash planned on releasing a triple LP, they were scheming The Clash Singles Bonanza in which they would dominate the year by continually releasing singles. In the end, they still put out enough music to release a new single every other week on the calendar, given most of side six was B-sides. While a lot of fans and writers dislike the final side of the album, some make exceptions for "Version City" since it is the only song on the sixth side of the record that isn't an alternate version of another song. Ironically, it's also a song that announces to the listener that everything that follows will be different *versions* of some of the previous songs by characterizing one of the most popular images in American music, a train. For The Clash, the train links them to a long musical tradition and also signifies a creative freedom to go wherever they want.

In blues music, trains are a symbol of African Americans during the Great Migration in the first half of the twentieth century traveling to cities like New York, Chicago, Detroit, and Pittsburgh to flee from the violence in the Deep South. Blues artists and other folk musicians would not only mention trains but use their guitars and voices to imitate the sound of a train or the blowing of a train whistle. Early rock 'n' roll guitarists, like Clash-touring-mate Bo Diddley, brought the train style shuffling of the guitar into the second half of the twentieth century to a new audience. In R&B and blues-based rock, the train continued to be used either lyrically or instrumentally to represent traveling either as an escape or for freedom. Not only is "Train in Vain" an R&B style Clash song, but the sound of a train can also be heard in "Police on My Back," and train tracks are featured prominently on the cover of *Combat Rock*. The train in "Version City" carries the great Mississippi Delta bluesmen to Chicago, picking up people at the crossroads and making stops at Syndrum Junction, Acapella Pass, Gibson Town, Fenderville, and Mesa Boogie Ranch. Next stop—some of the oddest tracks ever released by The Clash.

Living in Fame

Mikey Dread has appeared throughout *Sandinista!*, but in "Living in Fame" he is the primary singer. Strummer doesn't show up until the end to say "fuckin' 'ell, Mikey." This new version of "If Music Could Talk" seems to also be a freestyled track in which Dread's message is simple: bands need to live up to their name or end in shame. Dread shouts out 2-Tone ska bands The Selecter, The Specials, and Madness, before musing about The Clash and inserting Rasta themes, and calling out the Sex Pistols, Nipple Erectors, and Generation X. If the track serves any purpose, it's to give Dread a track all his own. Suppose they thought the groove was so nice that it had to appear twice.

Silicone on Sapphire

Paul Simonon admits that "Silicone on Sapphire" is a song he wouldn't have included on the album, saying he didn't understand the point of it. "To me it was just taking up space, but maybe puff-smoking people might find something to like about it."[8] At best, this dub version of "Washington Bullets" with a bunch of computer lingo foreshadows the rapid advancement of technology and personal computers in the 1980s and 1990s. Today, it sounds like a lesser version of Radiohead's "Fitter Happier." It doesn't help that the band has confused "silicon"—the chemical elements used in computer chips, and the namesake of Silicon Valley—with "silicone," the synthetic compound most associated with breast implants.

Version Pardner

A dub version of "Junco Partner," which already has a heavy reggae sound, "Version Pardner" is the same length as the original, but this time it's mostly an instrumental track with Strummer's extra heavy reverbed vocals winding in and out. *Is it necessary?* Probably not. But it's a genuine dub track that would undoubtedly give them some credibility from real deal dub and reggae artists. Of course, the credit belongs mostly to co-producer Dread. In fact, decades after the release of *Sandinista!*, Dread claimed that he hadn't been properly credited for his contributions to the album. That said, Dread believed that the issue was with the label instead of The Clash, clarifying, "The record company treat me with complete disrespect . . . But the group showed me nothing but respect."[9]

Career Opportunities

First appearing on their 1977 debut, "Career Opportunities" is one of the early Clash classics. In 1977, unemployment, especially for young adults, was a growing problem despite the Labour Party being in power. While unemployment was a major issue, what most offended Strummer was the opportunities available: office jobs, shopkeeper, assistantship, policeman, soldier, or RAF pilot. It was a live staple for the band in their early years that encapsulated the attitudes of the British punk scene. It's unclear why the version on *Sandinista!* has organ player Mickey Gallagher's kids on the record singing this punk rock anthem from only three years prior. One of the key differences is that the children add "I hate all of my school's rules / They just think that I'm another fool." The Clash revised the lyrics again on their 1982 recording *Live at Shea Stadium* (2008), changing "I don't want to go fighting in the tropical heat" to "Falklands Street" to adapt to the current Falkland Islands War. However, the inclusion of "Career Opportunities" during the Shea Stadium performance, in which they opened for The Who, was the ultimate sign of selling out their message to punks who believed The Clash no longer spoke for them. Nevertheless, the kid's version on *Sandinista!* is a reminder not to take everything too seriously.

Shepherds Delight

Coppola's *Apocalypse Now* is inspired by Joseph Conrad's 1899 book *Heart of Darkness*. Conrad's novel also inspired T.S. Eliot's 1925 poem "The Hollow Men," which is read by Colonel Kurtz, played by Marlon Brando, toward the end of the movie. "Shepherds Delight" begins with a low droning noise that sounds like a dying animal. The distressed sound fades and an acoustic-dub version of "If Music Could Talk" / "Living in Fame" begins. Higher-pitched animal wailing can be heard sporadically throughout the slight and easy groove. Without warning, the music ends and what sounds like a bomb being dropped interrupts the track until it fades into the album's final moments.

This is how *Sandinista!* ends
With both a bang and a whimper.

Conclusion

When it comes to the much-debated size of *Sandinista!*, even the members of The Clash were conflicted in hindsight. Topper Headon said of the massive thirty-six package, "I think it was a brilliant, incredible single album and a really, really good double album. But I think there's a lot of filler to make it a triple, personally."[1] With more time behind him, Strummer was more candid about discussing the length of the album, saying, "Many times I've debated with people about what should be on it, what shouldn't be on it. But, now looking back, I can't separate it. It's like the layers of an onion: there are some stupid tracks, there's some brilliant tracks. The more I think about it, the more happy I am that it is as it is."[2] To the surprise of critics and fans, time has been remarkably kind to the album's legacy. On *Rolling Stone*'s 2012 list of the 500 greatest albums, the album placed at 407. On the updated list in 2020, however, it managed to jump 84 spots to number 323. In 2018, *Pitchfork* ranked it the 144th best album of the 1980s. *Paste* listed it as the 46th best album of the 1980s in their 80 Best Albums of the 1980s in 2020.

The album was built to last. In fact, the excess of the album strengthens its longevity by offering more to revisit and discover over time. Suddenly, long overlooked tracks become personal favorites. More importantly, the larger themes of the album are still relevant today. Many of the album's first listeners heard about the people and the events it references for the first time in songs like "Washington Bullets." In fact, new listeners are still more likely to hear about Salvador Allende and Victor Jara from The Clash's 1980 album than they are in schools today because *Sandinista!* isn't just a collection of songs—it's a guide, a tool. Jones describes it as "a record for people who [are] on oil rigs or Arctic stations, and not able to get to record shops regularly. It [gives] them something to dip in and out of. Like a big book."[3] This is why *Sandinista!* demands and rewards relistening and engaging with a dense thirty-six-track magnum opus over six sides of vinyl—or better still, mixtapes and playlists.

In his fortieth anniversary tribute to *Sandinista!*, Rob Sheffield writes, "All six sides were a blast to explore—and argue over—but when it came to actual listening, everybody at the time just made a tape of their faves. Each fan's custom cassette was different . . . but that was part of the fun."[4] He adds that "Rebel Waltz" kicked off his mix and that it took a bar in Brooklyn that consistently played the album for him to appreciate side five. Similarly, Robert Christgau's original review recommends starting with *Sandinista Now!* but mentions that "Rebel Waltz" and "Something About England" are glaring omissions. In his book on The Clash, Sean Egan temporarily shifts the tone of his book with a compulsion to offer up his own twelve-track version of *Sandinista!* with picks that people would undoubtedly challenge as not being essential. A quick Reddit search reveals countless posts and links to blog sites of other fans volunteering their own take on how to remake *Sandinista!*

So far, this book has entertained the popular notion that the album would be better if it were condensed to a singular LP using the *Sandinista Now!* promo as the precedent, only to argue that the thirty-six songs that make up the triple LP are what make the album a master work. Though another great aspect of *Sandinista!*, and similarly large and ambitious LPs, is how listeners engage with the material. For nearly twenty-five years, fans of The Magnetic Fields' *69 Love Songs* (1999) have interacted with the triple CD by revisiting each song and taking it upon themselves to reconstruct the album for themselves and, more importantly, for others. *Sandinista!* has made it through the eras of vinyl, mixtapes, burned CDs, and shared playlists as a document that has been consumed, dissected, reimagined, reinterpreted, and repackaged by its audience.

These DIY versions of *Sandinista!* could be viewed as a neoliberal impulse to privatize the album and placing the individual consumer's demands ahead of the artist's intent. However, the triple LP format, and others like it, allow for dialogical and pluralistic criticism. In his 33 ⅓ book about Celine Dion's *Let's Talk About Love: A Journey to the End of Taste*, Carl Wilson examines the problem of musical taste. Wilson makes the case for pluralistic criticism, claiming it puts less stock in defending one's taste and more in depicting one's enjoyment.[5] People like Brad Efford took this to heart in 2014 when he created *The RS 500*, a site that ran for about five years with over a hundred writers who contributed personal pieces about the albums on the notorious list. Likewise, this book ends not with intellectual defenses of the album from the singular voice of the author but by enlisting the help of friends, writers, and musicians to share their own twelve-track version of *Sandinista!* It should be noted that none of the participants subscribe to the idea that the album should be reduced to one LP. Unsurprisingly, none of the lists are identical. Some have major omissions while others include tracks that will undoubtedly be puzzling to some. What the *Sandinista Now!* promo and these personalized twelve-track versions of the album reveal is that none of the reduced versions of the album are completely satisfactory, demonstrating the necessity of the album's expansive scope. Furthermore, exchanging the twelve tracks that mean the most to you with others reveals that these mixes offer a multitude of perspectives as to what makes *Sandinista!* a true masterpiece. Just as Wilson makes the case for a more dialogic criticism that asks, "here's my story, what's yours?"—this book ends with a question posed to *Sandinista!* fans new and old: here's my *Sandinista!*, what's yours?

Aaron Cohen

1. The Magnificent Seven
2. Something About England
3. Somebody Got Murdered
4. Up in Heaven (Not Only Here)
5. Corner Soul
6. Let's Go Crazy
7. Police on My Back
8. Washington Bullets

9. The Call Up
10. Broadway
11. Lose This Skin
12. Charlie Don't Surf

Randal Doane

1. The Magnificent Seven
2. Something About England
3. Somebody Got Murdered
4. Rebel Waltz
5. Junco Partner
6. Hitsville U.K.
7. One More Time
8. Up in Heaven (Not Only Here)
9. Police on My Back
10. Charlie Don't Surf
11. The Call Up
12. The Equaliser

Micajah Henley

1. The Magnificent Seven
2. Something About England
3. Rebel Waltz
4. Somebody Got Murdered
5. Up in Heaven (Not Only Here)

6. Corner Soul
7. The Call Up
8. Washington Bullets
9. Broadway
10. Charlie Don't Surf
11. The Street Parade
12. Shepherds Delight

Zeth Lundy

1. The Magnificent Seven
2. Hitsville U.K.
3. Something About England
4. Rebel Waltz
5. Somebody Got Murdered
6. One More Time
7. Up in Heaven (Not Only Here)
8. Police on My Back
9. The Equaliser
10. The Call Up
11. Lose This Skin
12. Charlie Don't Surf

Elizabeth Nelson

1. Police on My Back
2. Hitsville U.K.

3. Lose This Skin
4. The Sound of Sinners
5. The Magnificent Seven
6. Up in Heaven (Not Only Here)
7. Washington Bullets
8. Charlie Don't Surf
9. The Leader
10. Let's Go Crazy
11. Somebody Got Murdered
12. Something About England

Ryan Pinkard

1. Lightning Strikes (Not Once But Twice)
2. The Magnificent Seven
3. The Leader
4. Police on My Back
5. Something About England
6. Somebody Got Murdered
7. Up in Heaven (Not Only Here)
8. Let's Go Crazy
9. Washington Bullets
10. Charlie Don't Surf
11. Lose This Skin
12. The Sound of Sinners

Rob Sheffield

1. Police on My Back
2. Hitsville U.K.
3. Something About England
4. Rebel Waltz
5. Somebody Got Murdered
6. One More Time
7. Lightning Strikes (Not One But Twice)
8. Up in Heaven (Not Only Here)
9. The Call Up
10. Washington Bullets
11. Charlie Don't Surf
12. Career Opportunities

Rob Stone

1. The Magnificent Seven
2. Hitsville U.K.
3. The Leader
4. Somebody Got Murdered
5. Up in Heaven (Not Only Here)
6. Police on My Back
7. The Call Up
8. Washington Bullets
9. Lose This Skin

10. Charlie Don't Surf
11. The Street Parade
12. Version City

Luke Zerra

1. The Magnificent Seven
2. Hitsville U.K.
3. Ivan Meets G.I. Joe
4. Something About England
5. Somebody Got Murdered
6. Up in Heaven (Not Only Here)
7. The Sound of Sinners
8. Police on My Back
9. The Call Up
10. Washington Bullets
11. Charlie Don't Surf
12. Career Opportunities

Acknowledgments

I wrote this book from the comfort of my couch while being constantly cuddled or attacked by my cat Biscuit. When I wrote the proposal, I was an adjunct who spent the summer delivering food. Since then, I've continued to teach, worked a separate full-time job, had Covid, hosted multiple seasons of my podcast, bought a house, and gotten married. First, I'd like to thank my wife and perfect partner, Molly. Second, I'd like to thank my mom and sister. The rest appear in no particular order: Alyssa Januska-Solitro, Brad Efford, Brennan Taulbee, Carl Wilson, Casey Armington, Crissy Sans Robertson, Dane Ritter, David Johnson, Dominick Saragusa, Emily Tashjian Blanton, Jenny Glissman, Joy Wilkie, Lauren "Soup" Tashjian, Luanne Maguire, Luke Zerra, Lyn Bohyn, Max Scheidhauer, Michael Washburn, Morgan McKinley, Pam Freeman, Rob Stone, Shayne Druback, Spencer Darr, Tyler Scurlock, The Watsons, and Elizebeth and Ronnie from CD Central. I'd also like to acknowledge those who contributed their lists for the project: Aaron Cohen, Randal Doane, Zeth Lundy, Elizabeth Nelson, Ryan Pinkard, and Rob Sheffield. I've also been lucky to have incredible educators in my life. From Flagler College: Drs. Carl Horner, Mike Butler, Doug

McFarland, Darien Andreu, Tim Johnson, and Jack Daniels. From the University of Mississippi: Drs. Andy Harper and Ted Ownby. I'd also like to thank everyone at Bloomsbury Academic for making this possible. There are only a few bands that I can honestly say have been life changing. When I was given their debut album as a thirteen-year-old kid, The Clash changed my life and, unlike the others that have had a major influence on me, they continue to inspire me. Thus, a very special thanks to Joe Strummer, Mick Jones, Paul Simonon, and Topper Headon.

Notes

Introduction

1 Pete Holmes and Fred Armisen, "Fred Armisen," December 5, 2018, in *You Made It Weird with Pete Holmes*, Produced by Pete Holmes, podcast, MP3 audio, 2:24:41.

2 Sam Jones and Fred Armisen, "Fred Armisen: Life Lessons from 'The Clash,'" *Off Camera with Sam Jones*, May, 19, 2020, video, https://www.youtube.com/watch?v=wm-zkZISCU0.

3 Tony Fletcher, *The Clash: The Music That Matters* (New York: Omnibus, 2012), 51.

4 David Quantick, *The Clash* (New York: Thunder's Mouth Press, 2000), 55–7.

5 Sean Egan, *The Clash: The Only Band That Mattered* (New York: Rowman & Littlefield, 2015), 146.

The Politics of the Clash

1 Ernst Fischer, *The Necessity of Art: A Marxist Approach*, trans. Anna Bostock (Baltimore: Penguin Books, 1971), 8–9.

2 Peter Smith, "An Analysis of The Clash in Concert: 1977 to 1982," in *The Clash Takes on the World: Transnational Perspectives on The Only Band That Matters,* eds. Samuel Cohen and James Peacock (New York: Bloomsbury Academic, 2018), 30.

3 Andy Zieleniec, "Politics, Pastiche, Parody and Polemics: The DIY Educational Inspiration of The Clash," in *The Clash Takes on the World: Transnational Perspectives on The Only Band That Matters,* eds. Samuel Cohen and James Peacock (New York: Bloomsbury Academic, 2018), 61.

4 Fischer, *The Necessity of Art*, trans. Anna Bostock, 107.

5 Ibid., 88.

6 Ibid., 111.

7 Lloyd I. Vayo, "Turning Rebellion into Money: The Roots of The Clash," in *The Clash Takes on the World: Transnational Perspectives on The Only Band That Matters,* eds. Samuel Cohen and James Peacock (New York: Bloomsbury Academic, 2018), 79.

8 Chris Salewicz, *Redemption Song: The Ballad of Joe Strummer* (New York: Faber & Faber, 2007), 303.

9 Gregor Hall, *The Punk Rock Politics of Joe Strummer* (Manchester University Press, 2022), 11.

10 Ibid., 121.

11 Ibid., 16.

12 Ibid.

13 Ibid., 71.

14 Ibid., 94–5.

15 Ibid., 85.

16 Ibid., 82.

17 John Adams, "John Adams to Thomas Jefferson," August 24, 1815, *National Archives*, https://founders.archives.gov/documents/Jefferson/03-08-02-0560.

18 Gall, *The Punk Rock Politics of Joe Strummer*, 104.

19 Joh Berger, "Introduction: A Philosopher and Death," in *The Necessity of Art: A Marxist Approach*, Ernst Fischer, trans. Anna Bostock (Brooklyn: Verso Books, 2010), 3.

20 "Joe Strummer—Talks about Sandinista Lp, America, Finance, TOTPs & Image—Radio Broadcast 1981," September 17, 2019, https://www.youtube.com/watch?v=dAZvmt6-ArY&t=2s.

21 Ibid.

22 Fischer, *The Necessity of Art*, trans. Anna Bostock, 131–2.

23 Ibid., 114.

24 Ibid.

25 Ibid., 210.

26 Ibid., 193.

27 Ibid., 222–3.

28 "Joe Strummer—Talks about Sandinista Lp, America, Finance, TOTPs & Image—Radio Broadcast 1981." September 17, 2019, audio, https://www.youtube.com/watch?v=dAZvmt6-ArY&t=2s

29 Fischer, *The Necessity of Art*, trans. Anna Bostock, 114–15.

30 "The Clash—Audio Ammunition Documentary—Part 4—Sandinista," *Google Play*, September 10, 2013, video, https://www.youtube.com/watch?v=Bo56WJ-5uuM&t=5s.

The Making of Sandinista!

1 The Clash, *The Clash Book* (London: Atlantic Books, 2008), 110.

2 Ibid., 111.

3 Marcus Gray, *The Clash: Return of the Last Gang in Town* (London: Hal Leonard, 2004), 349.

4 Ibid., 350.

Part I

1 Robert Christgau, "The Clash: *Sandinista!* [Epic, 1981]," https://www.robertchristgau.com/get_album.php?id=3543.

Side One

1 The Clash, *The Clash Book* (London: Atlantic Books, 2008), 116.

2 Sean Egan, *The Clash: The Only Band That Mattered* (New York: Rowman & Littlefield, 2015), 143.

3 Ibid., 141.

4 Laurie Gunst, *Born Fi' Dead: A Journey Through the Jamaican Posse Underworld* (New York: Henry Holt, 1995), 111, 196.

5 The Clash, *The Clash Book*, 67.

6 Egan, *The Clash: The Only Band That Mattered*, 143.

7 James Henke, "The Clash: There'll Be Dancing in the Streets," *Rolling Stone*, April 7, 1980, https://www.rollingstone.com/music/music-news/the-clash-therell-be-dancing-in-the-streets-244087/.

8 Samuel Cohen and James Peacock, "Introduction: The Transnational Clash," in *The Clash Takes on the World: Transnational Perspectives on The Only Band That Matters*, eds. Samuel Cohen and James Peacock (New York: Bloomsbury Academic, 2018), 9.

9 Ibid., 11.

Side Two

1 Sean Egan, *The Clash: The Only Band That Mattered* (New York: Rowman & Littlefield, 2015), 28.

2 Ibid.

3 Samuel Cohen, "Washington Bullets: The Clash and Vietnam," in *The Clash Takes on the World: Transnational Perspectives on The Only Band That Matters*, eds. Samuel Cohen and James Peacock (New York: Bloomsbury Academic, 2018), 143.

4 *Joe Strummer: The Future Is Unwritten*, directed by Julien Temple (Vertigo Pictures, 2007).

5 Pat Gilbert, *Passion is a Fashion: The Real Story of The Clash* (Cambridge: Da Capo, 2005), 295.

6 Ibid., 114–15.

7 Chris Salewicz, *Redemption Song: The Ballad of Joe Strummer* (New York: Faber & Faber, 2007), 289.

8 Ibid.

Disc One

1 Pat Gilbert, *Passion is a Fashion: The Real Story of The Clash* (Cambridge: Da Capo, 2005), 283.

Disc Two

1 Pat Gilbert, *Passion is a Fashion: The Real Story of The Clash* (Cambridge: Da Capo, 2005), 136.

2 Joseph Maggs, "Fighting Sus! Then and Now," *Institute of Race Relations*, https://irr.org.uk/article/fighting-sus-then-and-now/.

3 Ibid.

4 The Clash, *Clash on Broadway* (1991), US: Legacy Recordings, 1991, CD.

Disc Three

1 Chris Salewicz, *Redemption Song: The Ballad of Joe Strummer* (New York: Faber & Faber, 2007), 84.

2 Ibid., 93.

3 Pat Gilbert, *Passion is a Fashion: The Real Story of The Clash* (Cambridge: Da Capo, 2005), 274.

4 The Clash, *The Clash Book* (London: Atlantic Books, 2008), 116.

5 Kurt Vonnegut, *Slaughterhouse-Five* (New York: Delacorte, 1969), 69–70.

6 Ernst Fischer, *The Necessity of Art: A Marxist Approach*, trans. Anna Bostock (Baltimore: Penguin Books, 1971), 8.

7 Salewicz, *Redemption Song*, 610.

8 The Clash, *The Clash Book*, 114.

9 Gilbert, *Passion is a Fashion*, 284.

Conclusion

1 The Clash, *The Clash Book* (London: Atlantic Books, 2008), 104.

2 Ibid., 108.

3 Ibid., 161.

4 Rob Sheffield, "In Praise of 'Sandinista!': Why the Clash's Triple-Album Mess Is Also Their Masterpiece," *Rolling Stone*, February 1, 2021, https://www.rollingstone.com/music/music-features/rob-sheffield-clash-sandinista-tribute-1121704/.

5 Carl Wilson, *Let's Talk About Love: A Journey to the End of Taste* (New York: Continuum, 2007), 157.

References

Adams, J. (1815), "John Adams to Thomas Jefferson, 24 August 1815," *National Archives*, Available Online: https://founders.archives.gov/documents/Jefferson/03-08-02-0560 (Accessed January 21, 2023).

Berger, J. (2010), "Introduction: A Philosopher and Death," in E. Fischer (ed.), *The Necessity of Art: A Marxist Approach*, trans. Anna Bostock, 1–14, Brooklyn: Verso Books.

Christgau, R. (1981), "The Clash: *Sandinista*!" Available Online: https://www.robertchristgau.com/get_album.php?id=3543 (Accessed May 11, 2021).

Clash on Broadway (1991), [Booklet] The Clash, US: Legacy Recordings.

Cohen, S. (2018), "Washington Bullets: The Clash and Vietnam," in S. Cohen and J. Peacock (eds.), *The Clash Takes on the World: Transnational Perspectives on The Only Band That Matters*, 131–46, New York: Bloomsbury Academic.

Cohen, S., and J. Peacock, eds. (2018), "Introduction: The Transnational Clash," in *The Clash Takes on the World: Transnational Perspectives on The Only Band That Matters*, 1–26, New York: Bloomsbury Academic.

Egan, S. (2015), *The Clash: The Only Band That Mattered*, New York: Rowman & Littlefield.

Fischer, E. ([1959] 1971), *The Necessity of Art: A Marxist Approach*, trans. Anna Bostock, Baltimore: Penguin Books.
Fletcher, T. (2012), *The Clash: The Music That Matters*, New York: Omnibus.
Gall, G. (2022), *The Punk Rock Politics of Joe Strummer*, Manchester: Manchester University Press.
Gilbert, P. (2005), *Passion is a Fashion: The Real Story of The Clash*, Cambridge: Da Capo.
Gray, M. (2004), *The Clash: Return of the Last Gang in Town*, London: Hal Leonard.
Gunst, L. (1995), *Born Fi' Dead: A Journey Through the Jamaican Posse Underworld*, New York: Henry Holt.
Henke, J. (1980), "The Clash: There'll Be Dancing in the Streets," *Rolling Stone*, April 7, 1980, Available Online: https://www.rollingstone.com/music/music-news/the-clash-therell-be-dancing-in-the-streets-244087/ (Accessed June 22, 2022).
Joe Strummer: The Future Is Unwritten (2007), [Film] Dir. Julien Temple, UK: Vertigo Pictures.
Maggs, J. (2019), "Fighting Sus! Then and Now," *Institute of Race Relations*, April 4, 2019, Available Online: https://irr.org.uk/article/fighting-sus-then-and-now/ (Accessed January 25, 2023).
Piccarella, J. (1981), "Sandinista!" *Rolling Stone*, March 5, 1981, Available Online: https://www.rollingstone.com/music/music-album-reviews/clash-sandinista-188352/ (Accessed May 11, 2021).
Quantick, D. (2000), *The Clash*, New York: Thunder's Mouth Press.
Salewicz, C. (2007), *Redemption Song: The Ballad of Joe Strummer*, New York: Faber & Faber.
Sheffield, R. (2021), "In Praise of 'Sandinista!': Why the Clash's Triple-Album Mess Is Also Their Masterpiece," *Rolling Stone*, February 1, 2021, https://www.rollingstone.com/music/music

-features/rob-sheffield-clash-sandinista-tribute-1121704/ (Accessed May 11, 2021).

Smith, P. (2018), "An Analysis of The Clash in Concert: 1977 to 1982," in S. Cohen and J. Peacock (eds.), *The Clash Takes on the World: Transnational Perspectives on The Only Band That Matters*, 27–44, New York: Bloomsbury Academic.

Strummer, J., M. Jones, P. Simonon, and N. Headon (2008), *The Clash*, London: Atlantic Books.

Vayo, L. (2018), "Turning Rebellion into Money: The Roots of The Clash," in S. Cohen and J. Peacock (eds.), *The Clash Takes on the World: Transnational Perspectives on The Only Band That Matters*, 65–80, New York: Bloomsbury Academic.

Vonnegut, K. (1969), *Slaughterhouse-Five*, New York: Delacorte.

Wilson, C. (2007), *Let's Talk About Love: A Journey to the End of Taste*, New York: Continuum.

Zieleniec, A. (2018), "Politics, Pastiche, Parody and Polemics: The DIY Educational Inspiration of The Clash," in S. Cohen and J. Peacock (eds.), *The Clash Takes on the World: Transnational Perspectives on The Only Band That Matters*, 45–64, New York: Bloomsbury Academic.

Also Available in the Series

1. *Dusty Springfield's Dusty in Memphis* by Warren Zanes
2. *Love's Forever Changes* by Andrew Hultkrans
3. *Neil Young's Harvest* by Sam Inglis
4. *The Kinks' The Kinks Are the Village Green Preservation Society* by Andy Miller
5. *The Smiths' Meat Is Murder* by Joe Pernice
6. *Pink Floyd's The Piper at the Gates of Dawn* by John Cavanagh
7. *ABBA's ABBA Gold: Greatest Hits* by Elisabeth Vincentelli
8. *The Jimi Hendrix Experience's Electric Ladyland* by John Perry
9. *Joy Division's Unknown Pleasures* by Chris Ott
10. *Prince's Sign "☮" the Times* by Michaelangelo Matos
11. *The Velvet Underground's The Velvet Underground & Nico* by Joe Harvard
12. *The Beatles' Let It Be* by Steve Matteo
13. *James Brown's Live at the Apollo* by Douglas Wolk
14. *Jethro Tull's Aqualung* by Allan Moore
15. *Radiohead's OK Computer* by Dai Griffiths
16. *The Replacements' Let It Be* by Colin Meloy
17. *Led Zeppelin's Led Zeppelin IV* by Erik Davis
18. *The Rolling Stones' Exile on Main St.* by Bill Janovitz
19. *The Beach Boys' Pet Sounds* by Jim Fusilli
20. *Ramones' Ramones* by Nicholas Rombes
21. *Elvis Costello's Armed Forces* by Franklin Bruno
22. *R.E.M.'s Murmur* by J. Niimi

23. *Jeff Buckley's Grace* by Daphne Brooks
24. *DJ Shadow's Endtroducing.....* by Eliot Wilder
25. *MC5's Kick Out the Jams* by Don McLeese
26. *David Bowie's Low* by Hugo Wilcken
27. *Bruce Springsteen's Born in the U.S.A.* by Geoffrey Himes
28. *The Band's Music from Big Pink* by John Niven
29. *Neutral Milk Hotel's In the Aeroplane over the Sea* by Kim Cooper
30. *Beastie Boys' Paul's Boutique* by Dan Le Roy
31. *Pixies' Doolittle* by Ben Sisario
32. *Sly and the Family Stone's There's a Riot Goin' On* by Miles Marshall Lewis
33. *The Stone Roses' The Stone Roses* by Alex Green
34. *Nirvana's In Utero* by Gillian G. Gaar
35. *Bob Dylan's Highway 61 Revisited* by Mark Polizzotti
36. *My Bloody Valentine's Loveless* by Mike McGonigal
37. *The Who's The Who Sell Out* by John Dougan
38. *Guided by Voices' Bee Thousand* by Marc Woodworth
39. *Sonic Youth's Daydream Nation* by Matthew Stearns
40. *Joni Mitchell's Court and Spark* by Sean Nelson
41. *Guns N' Roses' Use Your Illusion I and II* by Eric Weisbard
42. *Stevie Wonder's Songs in the Key of Life* by Zeth Lundy
43. *The Byrds' The Notorious Byrd Brothers* by Ric Menck
44. *Captain Beefheart's Trout Mask Replica* by Kevin Courrier
45. *Minutemen's Double Nickels on the Dime* by Michael T. Fournier
46. *Steely Dan's Aja* by Don Breithaupt
47. *A Tribe Called Quest's People's Instinctive Travels and the Paths of Rhythm* by Shawn Taylor
48. *PJ Harvey's Rid of Me* by Kate Schatz
49. *U2's Achtung Baby* by Stephen Catanzarite
50. *Belle & Sebastian's If You're Feeling Sinister* by Scott Plagenhoef
51. *Nick Drake's Pink Moon* by Amanda Petrusich
52. *Celine Dion's Let's Talk About Love* by Carl Wilson
53. *Tom Waits' Swordfishtrombones* by David Smay
54. *Throbbing Gristle's 20 Jazz Funk Greats* by Drew Daniel

55. *Patti Smith's Horses* by Philip Shaw
56. *Black Sabbath's Master of Reality* by John Darnielle
57. *Slayer's Reign in Blood* by D.X. Ferris
58. *Richard and Linda Thompson's Shoot Out the Lights* by Hayden Childs
59. *The Afghan Whigs' Gentlemen* by Bob Gendron
60. *The Pogues' Rum, Sodomy, and the Lash* by Jeffery T. Roesgen
61. *The Flying Burrito Brothers' The Gilded Palace of Sin* by Bob Proehl
62. *Wire's Pink Flag* by Wilson Neate
63. *Elliott Smith's XO* by Mathew Lemay
64. *Nas' Illmatic* by Matthew Gasteier
65. *Big Star's Radio City* by Bruce Eaton
66. *Madness' One Step Beyond…* by Terry Edwards
67. *Brian Eno's Another Green World* by Geeta Dayal
68. *The Flaming Lips' Zaireeka* by Mark Richardson
69. *The Magnetic Fields' 69 Love Songs* by LD Beghtol
70. *Israel Kamakawiwo'ole's Facing Future* by Dan Kois
71. *Public Enemy's It Takes a Nation of Millions to Hold Us Back* by Christopher R. Weingarten
72. *Pavement's Wowee Zowee* by Bryan Charles
73. *AC/DC's Highway to Hell* by Joe Bonomo
74. *Van Dyke Parks's Song Cycle* by Richard Henderson
75. *Slint's Spiderland* by Scott Tennent
76. *Radiohead's Kid A* by Marvin Lin
77. *Fleetwood Mac's Tusk* by Rob Trucks
78. *Nine Inch Nails' Pretty Hate Machine* by Daphne Carr
79. *Ween's Chocolate and Cheese* by Hank Shteamer
80. *Johnny Cash's American Recordings* by Tony Tost
81. *The Rolling Stones' Some Girls* by Cyrus Patell
82. *Dinosaur Jr.'s You're Living All Over Me* by Nick Attfield
83. *Television's Marquee Moon* by Bryan Waterman
84. *Aretha Franklin's Amazing Grace* by Aaron Cohen
85. *Portishead's Dummy* by RJ Wheaton
86. *Talking Heads' Fear of Music* by Jonathan Lethem
87. *Serge Gainsbourg's Histoire de Melody Nelson* by Darran Anderson

121. *Young Marble Giants' Colossal Youth* by Michael Blair and Joe Bucciero
122. *The Pharcyde's Bizarre Ride II the Pharcyde* by Andrew Barker
123. *Arcade Fire's The Suburbs* by Eric Eidelstein
124. *Bob Mould's Workbook* by Walter Biggins and Daniel Couch
125. *Camp Lo's Uptown Saturday Night* by Patrick Rivers and Will Fulton
126. *The Raincoats' The Raincoats* by Jenn Pelly
127. *Björk's Homogenic* by Emily Mackay
128. *Merle Haggard's Okie from Muskogee* by Rachel Lee Rubin
129. *Fugazi's In on the Kill Taker* by Joe Gross
130. *Jawbreaker's 24 Hour Revenge Therapy* by Ronen Givony
131. *Lou Reed's Transformer* by Ezra Furman
132. *Siouxsie and the Banshees' Peepshow* by Samantha Bennett
133. *Drive-By Truckers' Southern Rock Opera* by Rien Fertel
134. *dc Talk's Jesus Freak* by Will Stockton and D. Gilson
135. *Tori Amos's Boys for Pele* by Amy Gentry
136. *Odetta's One Grain of Sand* by Matthew Frye Jacobson
137. *Manic Street Preachers' The Holy Bible* by David Evans
138. *The Shangri-Las' Golden Hits of the Shangri-Las* by Ada Wolin
139. *Tom Petty's Southern Accents* by Michael Washburn
140. *Massive Attack's Blue Lines* by Ian Bourland
141. *Wendy Carlos's Switched-On Bach* by Roshanak Kheshti
142. *The Wild Tchoupitoulas' The Wild Tchoupitoulas* by Bryan Wagner
143. *David Bowie's Diamond Dogs* by Glenn Hendler
144. *D'Angelo's Voodoo* by Faith A. Pennick
145. *Judy Garland's Judy at Carnegie Hall* by Manuel Betancourt
146. *Elton John's Blue Moves* by Matthew Restall
147. *Various Artists' I'm Your Fan: The Songs of Leonard Cohen* by Ray Padgett
148. *Janet Jackson's The Velvet Rope* by Ayanna Dozier
149. *Suicide's Suicide* by Andi Coulter
150. *Elvis Presley's From Elvis in Memphis* by Eric Wolfson
151. *Nick Cave and the Bad Seeds' Murder Ballads* by Santi Elijah Holley